# The Professional Paralegal
# Job Search

D1308500

# The Professional Paralegal Job Search

## A Guide for Launching Your Legal Career

**Christofer Ulmont French**
Instructor and Career Development Counselor
Denver Paralegal Institute

**Little, Brown and Company**
**Boston   New York   Toronto   London**

Library of Congress Catalog No. 95-76233

ISBN 0-316-29436-5

EB-M

Published simultaneously in Canada
by Little, Brown & Company (Canada) Limited

Printed in the United States of America

# Summary of Contents

# Table of Contents

Contents

# About the Author

Christofer French is an instructor and Career Development Counselor at the Denver Paralegal Institute. He began his paralegal career in 1985, working as a paralegal for a sole practitioner. He moved to a medium-sized firm in Denver, handling the documents in a large multi-party case involving a defunct commercial development, and later joined one of the oldest law firms in the Rocky Mountain region. At DPI he is also in charge of the school's Outreach Program, where he comes into contact with a wide variety of firms.

# Introduction

This book is about finding and keeping a job as a paralegal. This new profession has grown every year since its beginning and now employs thousands of people from diverse backgrounds and experiences. Ambitious, hardworking paralegals are today working in professional situations of challenge and stimulation that they would only have imagined a few years ago.

Along with this tremendous growth came a corresponding expansion in paralegal job applicants—newly-educated paralegals, just like you. Those who have conducted effective paralegal job searches and are among the ranks of working paralegals can all attest that the legal profession embraces more kinds of backgrounds and a wider age group than any other profession. The downside of this success story is that placement challenges  exist and will most likely continue to exist. **Increased competition has made getting a paralegal job a professional endeavor all by itself.**

This book furnishes advice, tips, and tools that will help you get interviews and offers. The paralegal job search is a labyrinth you must make your way through, all the while avoiding some common pitfalls. For example:

- There are many sincere people who have the requisite earnestness and the basic qualifications, but they fail to become established as paralegals because they emphasize the wrong things in their cover letters, resumes, and interviews. Some who are in transition from previous professions are like generals who fight the last war: They often interview for their *last* job rather than the one they are interviewing for. The reality is that the paralegal profession requires some very particular skills and qualities along with the basic educational requirements. This book will help you package and present these skills and qualities. It also details the ways to keep your written presentation (resume, cover letter) out of your prospective employer's waste basket.
- It may surprise you to learn that advanced degrees, managerial expertise, and layers of supervisory experience can all become *negatives* if presented improperly. A similar mistake made during the job search is to assume that a diploma or certificate entitles you to an automatic entry-level placement. The diploma is waved at the

interview like a flag of victory, all the while you are overlooking that your education merely allowed you to sit in the interviewing chair! This book will help you position your qualifications to make the best impression and help you prepare for all kinds of inter- views—from the "friendly chat" to the "root canal interview."

- Many paralegal candidates harbor secret fears and worry needless- ly that they are too young or too old; underqualified, overquali- fied, or "other qualified"; the wrong sex, race, or age; or they are just not good enough to work in the paralegal profession. The marvelous truth is that this profession embraces all types, ages and backgrounds! And yet, this truth immediately strikes a warning chord: "With all of these potential paralegals from all kinds of backgrounds, how will I stand out?" This book will be your guide in determining which skills, strength, and personal qualities should be highlighted, and will teach you that you must come up with a positive and declarative way of promoting yourself.

Often, an unsuccessful job search can be attributed to one thing: You simply played your cards badly. This book will help you play your hand well, whatever it is. If you have a good hand, it will help you play it smart; if you have a weaker hand, it will give you strategies and help you achieve high standards so you can win.

After ten years in the legal arena, I have seen success stories aplenty along with tales of woe and disappointment. As a Career Development Counselor, I deal with the challenge of entry-level paralegal employment every day. Assisting and advising paralegal candidates and helping them get entry-level jobs is the continuing mandate of my career. Of course, no book can guarantee you the job you want—getting entry-level jobs is difficult. The goal of my book is to show you (1) how to put yourself in front of as many decision-makers as possible, and (2) how to make the strongest and most compelling presentation you can.

Those in the field know you must consciously build a career and take advantage of unexpected opportunities. Read the biographies in Appendix A, which detail the entry positions of three highly successful paralegals, and you will see that mastering the skill this book presents is a smart career move.

I wish to thank the reviewers listed below. Their careful efforts in reviewing the manuscript and their many thoughtful comments and suggestions are greatly appreciated.

Elizabeth Nobis
Lansing Community College

J. Lynne Wood
Anne Arundel Community

# Introduction

Dominic Latorraca
Arapahoe Community College

Paul Dusseault
Herkimer County
Comunity College

Joseph H. Moskowitz
Bergen Community College

Anna Durham Boling
Athens Area Technical Institute

# The Professional Paralegal Job Search

# CHAPTER 1

---

## *The Evolution of the Paralegal Profession*
### *What Is Defined by What It Is Not?*

### The Paralegal Profession: Heightened and Accelerated Evolution

Did you know that just a few short years ago, the term "paralegal" did not even exist? The evolution of the paralegal profession is marked by *speed*.

From the late 1960s through the 1990s, legal work has exploded in terms of size, dimension, and complexity. Think of the changes in American culture that have taken place since 1970: politics, law making, social change, case law, technology, philosophy, faxes, cellular phones, computers. The whole fabric of American culture has led to a tremendous growth in legal activity, and through it all the paralegal profession experienced a heightened and accelerated evolution. Paralegal utilization has now spread rapidly up and down the traditional legal profession and into all kinds of nontraditional or "alternative" settings. We won't go into all of the factors that caused the tremendous growth of legal activity of the last 30 years, but it is necessary for the trained paralegal to understand the world that he or she is entering and have the right tools to get there, stay there, and grow there.

The paralegal was "invented" or "created" in the 1970s, and a short 20 years later, the concept of trained paraprofessionals performing all kinds of legal work in a wide variety of legal settings has emerged. In the 1990s, there are paralegals in law firms doing the work that we normally associate with law firms: Bankruptcy (Creditor and Debtor), Corporate, Real Estate, Litigation, Workers' Comp, Insurance Defense, Medical Malpractice, Intellectual Properties, Entertainment Law, and Personal

1

Injury. In addition, there are paralegals working in departments of companies with vendors and contractors and franchisees, paralegals in Human Resource Departments, and paralegals employed by in-house corporate counsel for virtually any corporate entity that exists. To get a picture of where paralegals could find themselves, ask yourself, where are the lawyers? Where is the legal activity? The answer is, in American business, corporate, legal, private, and public activity. In short, "all over."

## What Is a Paralegal?

A paralegal is a nonlawyer who by virtue of training and experience provides legal support functions in law firms, governments, and other settings, subject to restrictions on the unauthorized practice of law. Many different labels identify individuals who lack membership in the bar but nevertheless carry out important legal functions. Paralegals usually undertake for attorneys such tasks as gathering and analyzing legal facts, performing legal research, drafting documents, and preparing witnesses and evidence for trial. However, what an individual paralegal actually does can vary widely. It depends on the employer, the kind of work involved, and the structure and philosophy of the organization.

The combined title—Paralegal Administrator, Paralegal Contract Supervisor, Paralegal Manager, Investigator Paralegal, Human Resource Paralegal—will continue to grow in number as backgrounds, skills, and particular pasts are married with the paralegal education and the paralegal experience. One reason for the rapid evolution in the paralegal profession is the way it takes almost any kind of past background, couples it with skills and experience and goals, and then emerges in some spot where formerly it had not been. (And then two to three more spring up in the first pioneer's place!)

Of the jobs that have been created in the last part of the twentieth century, most have highly defined parameters. Many are technical, and most have arisen from new technologies. The paralegal profession, however, is fundamentally different. It has arisen from an older profession, and its boundaries are defined more generally. What a paralegal does is often defined by what a paralegal must *not* do: sign pleadings, represent a client in court, or give "legal advice." Within ethical boundaries, you may do what a lawyer requests you to do. In fact, please anticipate what a lawyer will tell you to do, so that it can be finished when the lawyer asks for it.

By defining the paralegal profession by what it is not, we can see the infinite variety and scope of the field. In essence, the paralegal profession has experienced a tremendous horizontal growth pattern. Like a vigorous vine, the paralegal profession has grown from the law firm into corporations, government offices, state and local agencies, court systems, foundations, government contractors, manufacturing settings, and high-tech companies. The reasons for this growth all go back to that definition of what a paralegal is not. The unavoidable implication in the definition—the Rosetta Stone of paralegal growth and development—*Do the work.* Do not be a lawyer, but get trained and develop the skills that will enable you to do legal work. If it is helping set up corporations, do the work. If a lawyer needs help organizing and computerizing data for a 50,000-document case, do the work. If a sole practitioner needs help with a growing case load of domestic cases, roll up your sleeves and do the work. If a lawyer has run an ad in the Yellow Pages that is bringing in 20 bankruptcy cases a week, get hired, learn fast, and do the work. If a company needs help structuring settlements for insurance companies and law firms, get hired, and do the work.

## "I'd Like to Get One of Those!"—The Lawyer-Paralegal Relationship

As one attorney said to another upon meeting a third attorney buying lunch for her paralegal: "I'd like to get one of those." The initial job order for this first theoretical paralegal situation probably went something like this: "Do you know somebody else like you?"

All of the initial paralegal jobs were networked. They went out and found "someone like them." Who were they? "New Paralegals" told "Experienced Legal Secretaries" that there were jobs to be had that carried a new professional status. Both attorneys and new paralegals filled the ranks with existing associates and friends. They were from the world of law. They were coffee-break friends, coworkers, and past associates from other law firms. They were already qualified by experience, confidence, and professionalism in the law. They were known quantities. They came from existing legal and professional networks. **Trust and confidence are**  **of paramount importance in the world of law.** Clients place complete trust in their attorneys and that relationship. In a similar fashion, lawyers place tremendous confidence in their paralegals. As time passes the paralegal is relied upon more and more completely. This is why salaries and benefits are sometimes low in the beginning, but build quickly after a short time. When a lawyer's confidence and trust in you builds, and you become a valuable member of the team, your pay will reflect that trust.

Let us marvel a moment on the evolution of the paralegal profession — the profession for which you have been trained. As more and more paralegals have arrived on the scene, it has become very clear what a good paralegal is. Lawyers can use generalists. Even though many careers demand specialization, the new paralegal can be a declared generalist and not suffer for it. A liberal arts education can be very desirable! What has been called the "fastest growing profession" is today a profession that invites broad experience and a diverse background. In addition, lawyers benefit from paralegals with some professional experience. It is fine to be an ex-teacher or an ex-cop or restaurant manager or small business person. When a lawyer calls my office and asks for someone with common sense, what he or she is asking for is a little life experience, that is, someone who has a practicality about them. Lawyers do not simply require a "near lawyer" as a paralegal. **Lawyers want professionals with a broad array of skills who are flexible, adaptable, and willing to work hard (and sometimes long) hours to get the job done.** Special educational backgrounds are relished in specific practice areas, as long as you have a flexible professional approach. In fact, as I sit behind my career development desk a single message comes through all the job orders. They may all want lots of different things, but they also all want one thing: professionalism. They say, "I want someone who will double- and triple-check their work — put out a professional work product," or "I want someone who doesn't 'punch the clock.' If it takes 30 minutes or an hour extra to get a job done, I need a professional who will make sure the work is perfect and gets out the door in time."

So, a profession was born that required practical, skilled, well-trained support professionals who could use judgment and discrimination on a daily basis and apply all the tried and true work values and ethical standards that were needed to represent the law.

## The Law Firm: Where Paralegals Originated

Let us go back and consider the structure in which the paralegal profession was born — the firm. The law firm will always have an impact on how you function in the paralegal world. Its original structure carried the paralegal in a *staff relationship,* not a *line function.* From the beginning, it was clear that paralegals would be self-directed professionals providing support work. They would not be giving orders to subordinates, but rather be entrusted with projects over which they would be responsible. Since paralegals are by definition not lawyers, the work divides itself quite easily. Attorneys are the planners, strategists, directors; paralegals are the technicians, organizers, fact experts, custodians of details. The paralegal plays a distinctly different role than the lawyer, and you must recognize your value as an individual with unique skills within the structure of the law firm.

## But I managed 25 people in my old job!

 As you seek a paralegal position, the lesson to be learned from the law firm structure is: **You must bring your skills, not your titles.** Many people have uttered variations on the phrase, "But I managed 25 people in my old job!" with complete conviction and wonder, after I told them to "sell your skills, not your titles." We will address the issue of transferability of skills in later chapters, but you must keep in mind that the paralegal profession was created for the practical reasons of *workload*—to get the job done as efficiently as possible. Your rank and title in a previous job are irrelevant in the search for a paralegal position. What you can do, not who you were, is what matters. Likewise, the profession is not organized hierarchically. You will not find five levels of paralegal. You do not get battlefield commissions or suddenly have "vice president" placed after your name. You are what you are by virtue of the work you do, your reputation, and your achievements.

## Diplomacy 101: The law firm environment

Diplomacy 101 is not a course suggestion for a paralegal program, though it might be a good idea for a seminar. Because paralegals are not part of a managerial/administrative structure, they must stand on their own. Paralegals should have the diplomatic skill to negotiate themselves through the perils of law firm gossip, relationships, who's in, who's out, and all the problems that arise in a stressful, tense, and sometimes seething subsurface political environment. The paralegal who fails to recognize the importance of secretaries is sometimes in as much danger as one who disappoints a senior partner. The need for diplomacy is made obvious not only by the nature of the work being done, but also where it is being done.

What more can be added to this basic description of the paralegal's role? The first paralegals had skill and adaptability. These two elements are further reinforced by the firm's structure itself. In the firm, since you are standing on your own, you should have as many technical skills as you can possibly develop. Diplomacy is also an important skill, for you will need friends. You will have to be adaptable, especially in the beginning, for it is adaptability that gets careers going. Many specialists were once volunteers who decided to take on a special case for which they had no experience. Their willingness to pitch in and help allowed them to gain valuable knowledge.

Adaptability is an asset that will help you work with the one entity that stands responsible for everything that a paralegal touches—the *lawyer*. The lawyer/paralegal partnership is one of complementary opposites: Strategy vs. Technicality, Overview vs. Detail Analysis, Plan vs. Execution. The challenge of dealing with a lawyer comes from the fact that the paralegal must adapt to the style of the attorney. While paralegals are adapting, they must also keep intact their self-esteem and enthusiasm. The paralegal, as adaptor and professional, must be able to rise above the immediate hectic dramas of the law office.

Working with lawyers is what paralegals do. The excitement and challenge of working in the traditional law firm has to do with the high stakes of legal activity, the well-developed egos that populate the world of law, the tense deadline-orientation that pushes everything forward and then occasionally leaves you becalmed on a quiet sea of inactivity. When a case settles and the firm throws a big party, you suddenly have nothing to do—when the hour before you were being driven to distraction by a score of unfinished assignments. You pop the champagne instead of the aspirin bottle and smile to yourself because you are working in a pretty exciting world. Lawyers are a part of this world, and so are you. You are in a law firm, that sometimes sedate and serene place of thick carpet and serious looks that can in a given situation turn into a place of high drama, hilarity, confusion, or pure adrenalin-driven fun.

## Here to Stay: Paralegals in Law Firms and Nontraditional Settings

Even though there are still firms that say, "We do not use paralegals," in cities large and small the paralegal is now a permanent part of the traditional law firm. Some firms have stylized their practice around paralegals. One particular estate planning and probate practice instituted a well-organized system of small teams of attorneys matched with a cadre of paralegals and sophisticated computers. Their ratio is one attorney to three paralegals. In other firms the ratio is three or four lawyers to one paralegal. In some firms it is ten to one. Places where paralegal use is minimal or nonexistent await that one experimental day when a stubborn old attitude gives way to a begrudging mumbled statement: "Well, I guess we'll hire you, just to see; now this is an experiment, mind you . . . we'll have a 90-day probational period . . . then we'll sit down and talk again."

Within this quiet acceptance lies the key to paralegal success. Well-trained, skillful, enthusiastic professional paralegals have found themselves in this scenario tens of thousands of times. More often than not, after 90 days the paralegal became a "part of the woodwork." When paralegals get a chance to prove their usefulness they not only carve out a job for themselves, they change workloads and expand practice areas. They increase profits. Though not carrying the prestige of the lawyer's status, you, as a paralegal, can have rightful pride and self-respect in knowing that you are a member of a new profession that is influencing the American legal system in many ways. The status of paralegals in the law firm is fixed.

The "alternative" career or the nontraditional paralegal is a recent phenomenon in the United States. Today, paralegals work in foundations, factories, courthouses, state legislative agencies, city governments, racing and gambling commissions, software companies, research laboratories, and federal bureaucracies. They can be found working everywhere. From manufacturing to service, from transportation to construction, from industry to the professions there is a potential legal fact directly or indirectly involved every time the sun rises. As the department head of a major corporation confided to me over the phone, "I'm not sure what I'm looking for, but I think it's a paralegal."

There are no job openings in this profession, like there are openings for a spot on a production line. **Paralegal employment situations are probably better described as** *opportunities,* **or better yet,** *windows of opportunity.* This is a prime concept in your overall professional development. *Networking* is a word that you will continue to hear over and over as years go on. It is one of the main ways your professional development will continue *after* you obtain your entry level paralegal employment.

## Importance of Job Search Skills

Academic achievement and successful job searching are separate skills. The most brilliant paralegal in the world who cannot employ basic job search skills will most probably be unemployed. The most average academic achiever in your class could be the most effective job search professional and thus the most happily employed paralegal in your class. This book will outline and instruct you on the elements you need to obtain and maintain professional paralegal employment at the entry level and beyond.

Excellent academic skills
Demonstrate themselves in the Report Card.
Many attributes show themselves in
Social Approval, Peer Recognition and Popularity . . .
But alas . . .
Well-developed Professional Job Search Skills
Only show themselves
In Employment.

# CHAPTER 2

## The World of the Working Paralegal
### Job Expectations and Descriptions

*Our plans miscarry because they have no aim. When a man does not know what harbor he is making for, no wind is the right wind.*
Seneca (4 B.C.-65 A.D.)

*If it looks like a duck, acts like a duck and sounds like a duck, . . . it's probably a duck!*
Traditional

You must know what harbor you are making for to find employment as a paralegal. The first challenge is to know what winds will take you to what jobs.

Paralegals must understand what it is they will be working at and what they will be doing after they are hired. Those engaged in a paralegal job hunt must master a special language that is derived from the various modes of legal employment you will encounter during your search. Often, those who fail to achieve employment have failed to understand the language of the paralegal job descriptions that were discussed in their interviews.

## Assumptions, Expectations, Apprehensions, and Misinformation

Nothing dims the prospect of success like going into a new job with a head full of bad information, wishful thinking, questionable assumptions, and unrealistic expectations. You may have assumptions and expectations that are based upon any number of sources, all of which could contain a mix of accuracy and inaccuracy. In describing practice areas and jobs, we will discuss how much time is spent on word processing, in public contact, in "the back room" handling involved research projects or large litigation support tasks, or on the phone. It is important to know not only what legal activity you will be working on, but also how your time will be divided. Those who become working paralegals do not:

♦ talk about how much they love public contact when they will be doing multidocument litigation support
♦ emphasize their high grades in legal research when they interview to do client intake for a bankruptcy practice
♦ talk about how they have always wanted to "save the environment" to a firm representing a chemical company

 **Put your assumptions "on hold" until you find out about the basics of your prospective firm.**
Is the firm:

♦ plaintiff's practice or defense?
♦ large or small?
♦ general or specialized?
♦ an employer of a large number of paralegals or a small number?
♦ sophisticated in its use of paralegals or basic?
♦ a heavy user of computers or computerphobic?
♦ one that grants paralegals public contact or little public contact?
♦ one that considers paralegals part of the professional staff or the nonprofessional staff?

## Query, Query, Query

I do not intend to offer an exhaustive source of all paralegal job descriptions, but instead to give you an understanding of just how much different paralegal jobs will vary. This will hopefully raise your consciousness during the job search process so that you will "query, query, query." Keep your antennae out for key points about the particular working world you are trying to join. Figure 2-1 gives you an overview of the different opportunities available to paralegals. As you can see, paralegal skills are useful in a wide variety of settings. Find out about the specific job description for which you are applying and be sure the job meets your expectations.

For example, some paralegals want (and even crave) client contact. Others become paralegals so they do not have to deal with clients at all. One paralegal job may emphasize client contact and the other may virtually forbid it. It depends on the attitude of the boss, the community in which you live, the practice area, and whether the job involves the defendant or the plaintiff. (Remember, this is just a particular example that points up the need for you to use this chapter in your quest for employment.) Know what you are likely to get when you go hunting for it. Be sure to ask all you can about it before accepting it. And then once you have accepted a job, find out even more about it, and then fully embrace the job as it is given to you.

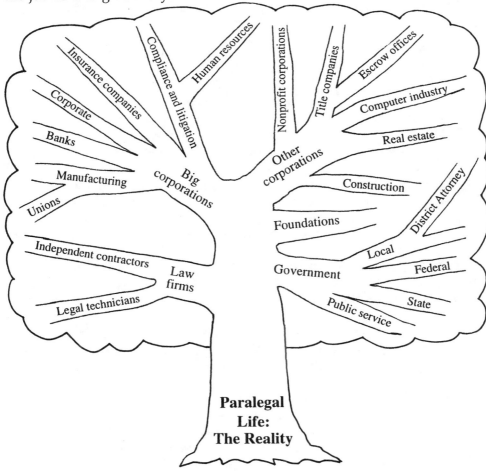

**Fig. 2-1** Paralegal employment.

## The Real World of the Paralegal

Before describing specific practice areas and focusing on paralegal duties within those practice areas, a look at the "real world" picture would be appropriate. Most paralegals are multiple or (general) practice area paralegals for two reasons:

1) Many law firms start out with generalist practices and grow to become specialists. Thus they need paralegals who can help in different areas.
2) Many specialist paralegals have grown into those categories *after* being exposed to a wide range of practice areas.

The fact that many paralegals are generalists goes straight to job search issues:

| | |
|---|---|
| *Flexibility* | Willingness to handle differing tasks in the same day |
| *Adaptability* | Able to move skillfully and enthusiastically from basic to complex, team to individual tasks |
| *Enthusiasm for new assignments* | Take on the unknown with a sense of adventure; embrace the new |
| *Willingness to develop new skills* | Always ready to learn new software, research a new topic, delve into a new practice area; in short, do what's needed, even if it has not been handled before |

 **Be interested in the employer's stated practice areas. Be enthusiastic about potential new assignments. The natural evolution of practice areas and firm development will tend to make you a multiple-practice-area paralegal.**

In a five-year paralegal career, I handled many practice areas. In my first job, which lasted one year, I was hired to handle a basic plaintiff's bankruptcy practice, which grew into three other practice areas.

**Job #1**

| | |
|---|---|
| *Original Role* | Bankruptcy Paralegal |
| *Actual Role* | Bankruptcy Paralegal, Domestic Relations Paralegal, Estates/Wills/Trusts Paralegal, Criminal Defense Paralegal |

I left for a substantial pay increase to Job #2. At the second firm, the firm started with one paralegal (myself) and in a two-and-one-half year period grew to three additional attorneys and five more paralegals. The number of practice areas demonstrate the firm's rapid expansion.

**Job #2**

| | |
|---|---|
| *Original Role* | Products Liability/Personal Injury Paralegal (Asbestos cases) |
| *Actual Role* | Products Liability/Personal Injury Paralegal, Mechanic's Lien Foreclosure Paralegal, Domestic Paralegal, Criminal Defense Paralegal, Bankruptcy Paralegal (Creditor), Lender Liability Paralegal, Litigation Paralegal |

This firm's partnership broke up, and I went on to a large law firm in Job #3. In this position, I was brought on to handle one large litigation case involving tens of thousands of documents. When that case was settled I went on to handle other cases in various practice areas.

**Job #3**

| | |
|---|---|
| *Original Role* | Litigation Support Paralegal |
| *Actual Role* | Lit Support Paralegal, Lender Liability Paralegal, Commercial Paralegal, Intellectual Properties Paralegal, Personal Injury/Insurance Defense Paralegal |

This brief outline of my paralegal career is very representative of the way law firms work. A paralegal is "on board" and, like a ship at sea, all hands contribute to the whole effort. It is not generally in a paralegal's self-interest to refuse work because of one's classification, even though in larger firms there is a "division of labor," and specialist paralegals are usually busy at their special practice, be it bankruptcy, foreclosures,  litigation, corporate law, etc. **Before specific paralegal duties are outlined, you must understand that any given paralegal may do one, two, three, four, or more of these job descriptions in any given year or in any given stay at a particular law firm or over the course of a career. It is a rare person indeed who is hired to do one particular job and then continues in that specialty area over a number of years.**

## *Cultivating personal and professional viability*

One other factor should be mentioned before we delve into the specialties. With the modern law firm and the nature of work flow being what they are, it behooves the working paralegal to have as broad an experience as possible while still maintaining an area of strength. Being able to say you have a strength or specialty is very important, but it is also helpful to be able to say you have had exposure to two or three other practice areas. Job leads are often accompanied with statements like: "I want a two-year paralegal with any kind of law office experience, and whatever Workers' Comp or personal injury experience they can muster up."

So as you proceed through this chapter, remember that if you fall in love with one practice area, you still have to be a useful member of a firm. Educate yourself, ask questions, and test out different job descriptions to see if they match your personality profile and work style. At the same time, stay flexible, be informed, and be ready to roll up your sleeves and handle tasks no matter what the practice area.

## The Litigation Paralegal

One student recently asked me, "When people say 'litigation,' they're not talking about practice areas are they? . . . They're talking about the process of settling the dispute, whatever that dispute is. . . . Right?"

Yes. The *litigation paralegal* is a paralegal who assists attorneys in the formalized settling of a controversy between two or more parties. Civil litigation involves many subject areas. The issues could be contracts, a car wreck, an abandoned commercial development, a bankruptcy and foreclosure, a contractual dispute between an agent and a rock band, a commercial conflict between several parties, medical malpractice, torts of all kinds, and any other dispute that is settled in the courtroom.

You can safely assume that as a paralegal, you will encounter litigation in your career. To know what lawyers are seeking in a paralegal, you can just look at what happens in the litigation process and find important clues. This is why we will delve into the litigation process.

The first thing to be said for the litigation process and the paralegal's role in it is that it is varied. It is stimulating to move from one subject matter to another, or to work with documents that may range from deeds of trust to mechanic's liens to wills to scribbles on a paper napkin to diaries, calendars, and love letters. It is the litigation paralegal who often gets first plugged in to database management and has to use one or two of several software programs (DBase IV, Paradox, Q&A, Lotus, and many others).

## Database management

If you have no experience with any of the preceding software programs or others like them, be enthusiastic about the prospect of learning them when you become employed. Even better, figure out a way to get trained on these programs so that you can include them on your resume. The entry-level paralegal who can boast of this kind of experience has an advantage over other job candidates.

Several years ago, I was asked to begin performing data entry on a mechanic's lien case that had just been filed near Vail, Colorado. Two years and 75 defendants later, a small building was rented to house all of the documents that were generated in this suit. Inquisitive enthusiasm kept me on the case. By time of trial, I had become the "fact expert" on the failed multi-million dollar complex construction project. The use of computers had not reached the height of sophistication that it has today, but in that case (as in all cases) I started with a willingness to use the computer to my advantage, even if my "computer literacy" was not too high. Document imaging and other high-tech approaches to document management may be in store for us in the near future, but no matter what happens in litigation, there will always be a need for a talented, skilled, and enthusiastic litigation paralegal who is willing to become friendly with and talented in document management.

In cases that involve thousands or even hundreds of thousands of documents, whole teams can be involved. Some cases require only a few boxes of documents, while some class action suits have documents housed in warehouses and buildings, coded and labeled by floor, section, row, and box. In these latter cases, trained paralegals may be doing:

1) document labeling
2) document coding
3) data entry
4) quality control (checking others' work)
5) document organization and indexing
6) liaison with computer consultants and attorneys
7) report production
8) personnel supervision and team leading
9) document reproduction

As a litigation paralegal, you may work in certain practice areas or firms that never require this kind of massive organizational effort, but the real point here is that **the litigation paralegal is in charge of** *document retrieval,* **no matter how small the case. Some cases may only have 20 to 30 documents, but if the files are poorly organized and discovery is handled haphazardly, even those documents can become a problem for a paralegal.**

You will be held responsible for the state of the documents involved in a litigated matter. If you are not given responsibility over the files, try to get that responsibility. A secretary who is managing the files may be happy to allow you take over that aspect of his or her job. If they view it as a treasured area of responsibility, ask if you can involve yourself in the indexing and labeling.

> If you will be held responsible for it, try to take control of it.

> **The Law of Document Blindness:** When an attorney is standing at the door—red-faced, perspiring, with a strained countenance and a raspy voice—pleading for a certain key document, the optic nerve of the paralegal will become blind to the particular document requested, especially if that document is not in its proper place in the file because it is in the paralegal's right hand.

The Law of Document Blindness is an exaggeration of the state of affairs in a busy law office. Still, it is the litigation paralegal's absolute job requirement numero uno to not only label and index documents (or be responsible for this) but to be able to retrieve them quickly.

## Anatomy of a lawsuit

When civilization took the step of having judges or local authorities decide matters of dispute, and people stopped using axes and guns and fists to settle their differences, the lawsuit became the way to formalize this battle. Some may frown on analogies to wars, but in fact that is what disputes would become without litigation. Since litigation is the main focus for a great percentage of paralegals in the country, it is important for all paralegals to understand the anatomy of a lawsuit, from initial interviewing, investigating, and fact finding, to the preparation of demand letters, complaints, and initial discovery, to the flurry of responsive pleadings, answers, and cross-complaints, to discovery motions, depositions, exhibit preparation, and trial preparation. A paralegal can be involved from the first interview to appeal.

Ideally, the paralegal is brought in as early as possible in the case. The reality is that when you are hired, cases will be in all stages of maturity: just beginning, just ending, somewhere in the middle. It is always important therefore to emphasize qualities like "fast learner" or "quick study" or "eager to learn new material" during the job interview.

### Interviewing and Investigating

The initial phase of a lawsuit is spent gathering information, finding facts, determining issues, and orienting the dispute. You sit down and determine all the potential sources of information and evidence. Places, institutions, names, addresses, businesses, and locations will become paramount as you begin to create a fact pattern of information. Paralegals in the beginning of a lawsuit will contact hospitals, law officers, public entities containing records (from heating bills to criminal records), secretaries of state, county sheriffs, attorney generals' offices, businesses, individuals, and any person or entity which could hold information or evidence. Recordkeeping, tracking details, and following through are all important talents to emphasize during the interview.

Skip tracing (the act of finding people who don't want to be found) and directory searching are good skills to have. Fill your Rolodex with phone numbers. In the beginning, get help from fellow workers. Remember, you do not have to reinvent the wheel—people in your firm will have done investigation before, so use them as a resource.

Early on, think about how you will number and classify your case documents. Look at some old case files and study how they have been organized and broken down. Use old systems if they work well. Do not be too much of a pioneer when it comes to file organization systems, but at the same time, if you are in charge and responsible, make your system as effective as possible.

### Begin Summaries, Memos, Chronologies, and Docketing Systems

There is nothing more visually effective than an early layout or graphic display of a case to give you a grasp of the issues and facts. Do not get too fancy or spend extra money unless requested to, but formalizing and ordering information in outlines, chronologies, simple graphs, and diagrams is a professional and thorough way of grappling with a new case.

Become familiar with your state's rules of civil procedure and discovery. If your firm has a computerized docketing system, insert your case into that system and keep your own docketing file for the case. Go through the complaint and the answer and determine the initial deadlines. As discovery orders are established, enter those dates on your docket; as motions are filed, enter response dates and dates for replies when necessary. Docket for your side *and* the other side. *You should know when they are late!* And you most certainly should prevent your side from making late filings by way of friendly memos. An organized paralegal will draft a memo once a month just to verify and confirm dates. *When* is a supreme issue in the law. Recording *when*, and knowing when *when* changes, and recording and knowing the new *when*, all fall to the paralegal. Certainly attorneys are endlessly concerned about *when*, but this is an area in which you as a paralegal can shine. In litigation, "when" is as important as "what." From statutes of limitation to filing appeals, "when" is always entwined in the story line, and you as a paralegal are in the middle of the whole scheme.

As the file grows and the case proceeds, write, send, and file status reports on a regular basis. You will keep yourself up on the case as dates, times, and issues arise. Status reports will keep you continually aware that "the wheels of Justice grind slowly, but they grind exceedingly fine." The pace of the law is like an ax grinding grain on a stone. When things are quiet, it can be downright dull. But when a deadline arrives, you must be the one ringing the bell.

> Words a paralegal should never say:
> *"Oh, was that today?"*

### Research and Writing

In Chapter 5, we will discuss the way your written presentations (resumes and cover letters) become the way you are judged and measured. So, too, your oral presentations (interviews and phone contacts and networking) are statements about you, your professionalism, and your education. In much the same way, your memos, correspondence, reports, and drafting all reflect upon you. People form strong negative and positive images of others *before* they meet them, by way of their *work product*. Take care to write clearly and well. Organize your thoughts. Do not carelessly frame your written communications. You will be judged by them.

### Discovery

Hopefully, you will be involved in the formulation of the discovery plan. With new rules of discovery on the scene, be aware of local adaptations and permutations in your state and understand the rules regarding discovery. You will be asked to assist in the preparation of requests for admissions, production of documents, interrogatories, and discovery motions. You will certainly be involved in organizing, assembling, reviewing, and labeling documents pertaining to these matters.

Create witness files, and file every single communication you have with those witnesses in those files. Paralegals are often asked to meet with clients and assemble all client documents. It is at this time when you will get a look at privileged documents and documents that will fall under relevancy questions.

As documents are produced you will see an astonishing array of filing that will automatically be created. New rules are designed to simplify document production and discovery issues, but it still lies at the paralegal's door to know:

- what documents came to us from them and when
- what documents were *not* sent to us when requested by us
- what documents were sent to them and when
- what documents were *not* sent to them and why
- what further information would be important to know

### Depositions

Depositions are complicated because you are attempting to stage pretrial get-togethers in which everyone must be represented. Depositions are crucial because they can be used as evidence, and they can be fraught with tension. But when someone does not show up, the pretrial get-together must be canceled, and everyone is irritated. So there is much work for the paralegal here. First, the initial work is all on the phone. Everyone must agree on times and places and participants. Then . . .

1) prepare subpoenas and notices of deposition
2) help draft potential deposition questions
3) attend depositions (if requested) and take notes
4) get copies of depositions and summarize them according to firm/attorney format
5) follow up on need for depositions with attorneys as deadlines approach

If interstate travel is involved, all of these previous points become even more problematic. Logistics is everything with depositions. Remember: Original Depositions must be kept and filed for potential use in trial.

### Pretrial

In the pretrial phase, paralegals start to really earn their keep. Pressure builds to focus on key testimony. Perhaps last-minute depositions need to be summarized. Summaries of key witness testimony may be demanded and an initial trial exhibit list will be forming from deposition exhibits, affidavits, expert witnesses, and interviews. The paralegal becomes deeply involved with filing Disclosure Certificates and Trial Data Certificates (pretrial certificates), and could be attending hearings, conferences, and settlement meetings. If so, you will be taking notes and, later, preparing follow-up materials.

The preparation of special demonstrative exhibits often falls to paralegals. At this time, *many* duties fall to you. Attorneys count on paralegals to stay in touch with clients and take care of loose details and follow-up items. They look to them for advice about the psychology of certain approaches in testimony, or exhibits, or lines of argument. Often they are not looking for an "expert's opinion" as much as for a fresh (but informed) point of view. Remember that you will be relied on to be a professional and a steady force as trial nears.

### Trial Notebooks and Trial Exhibits

These special areas of strong paralegal activity are a "work in progress" all the way up until deadline. You must be sure to prepare them with care and according to instruction — this is no time for Amateur Hour. Assemble them with all of the best office materials you can get.

Trial notebooks are intended to be an outline of the sequential presentation of the case. Attorneys will tell you what should go in, but you should be armed with your lists, indexes, and summaries so that you will be able to help. Paralegals exhale with fatigue when the subject of trial notebooks comes up, not because they are intellectually impenetrable masterpieces, but because the *time* issue is most always involved, and then along with that there are *sudden changes*. These two elements make the paralegal's role very important. Be assured that the firm notes the effort that goes into late night episodes and shortened or obliterated lunch (and dinner) hours. (Overtime in many cases is paid in these situations.)

### Settlement or Trial

Your responsibilities in trial will vary widely. Some paralegals enjoy "second chair" kinds of responsibilities. Some are not involved at all. If you do get to participate in a trial, prepare yourself emotionally. Be ready to concentrate and to experience intense feelings. Some trials can be tedious, but others can really be the fulfillment of months of anticipation.

Remember, all of these litigation processes can be arrested at any time by a *sudden settlement*. The build-up before trial is exhausting for all concerned. Mentally, emotionally, physically, and psychologically you become geared up. The whiplash that a settlement can cause on trial preparation momentum is tremendous. If settlement does occur, you will not be left without work; they may have you assist with the settlement agreements and releases, and work on stipulations and motions. But all through the litigation process, settlement talk can be heard:

"There's no way this is going to settle."

"I can't believe they won't settle."

"What I could do with half a million."

This kind of talk should not keep you from preparing like you are going to have to go to trial when it is scheduled. At trial, if you are given a full complement of assignments, you will be involved in all or parts of the following:

1) subpoena preparation
2) voir dire assistance
3) jury instructions drafting
4) witness and expert "stage management"
5) taking notes and tracking of exhibit numbering and rulings during trial
6) meetings about strategy and witnesses

Though not all paralegals can sit "second chair" at a trial, there are those who have done so, and the drama can be truly stimulating. The whole process of being involved in a trial from precomplaint days to posttrial and appeal can take years and hold a bundle of exciting memories and unforgettable images.

### Posttrial

Sometimes you can feel that a case will never go away. The appeals process can truly give you that sense. You should be prepared to summarize trial testimony from your notes, help with posttrial motions, and work with the bills and costs.

Do not forget to go straight to your Rules and schedule a timetable for the appeals process. Research may be in order if requested. You may be asked to assist with briefs, Shepardizing, and other matters, such as the designation of appeal and the drafting of the notice of appeal.

## *Observations about the litigation process*

Litigation includes every practice area, and specialty practice areas, such as Bankruptcy, Real Estate and numerous other categories, share some common elements. That is why many of the observations made about the litigation paralegal can and do apply to all paralegals. The issue of *time* is ubiquitous in the law. A paralegal who neglects issues of time in *any* practice area will suffer. Organization and scheduling and document retrieval are also universally applicable to all paralegals. Further discussions about paralegal positions in various specialty areas and practices will focus more on the specifics of that job, but keep in mind that all paralegal jobs are concerned with schedules, filing dates, and due dates; that all paralegal jobs focus on documentation (its acquisition, labeling, organization, indexing, and quick retrieval). This may sound too obvious, but many graduates of paralegal programs get focused on grades, legal theory, issue argumentation, and the hustle and bustle of a busy job—and forget the basics. This they do at their peril.

Let us look at some basic paralegal job descriptions from other areas of discipline to observe their differences and similarities.

# The Bankruptcy Paralegal

## *Working for the debtor*

A good representative entry-level paralegal job could be in the office of a sole practitioner who deals with bankruptcy law and domestic law. Fifty to ninety percent of such a practice could be in bankruptcy. Many advertise in the Yellow Pages and take in mostly Chapter 7's (debtor). In this position a paralegal in such an office will do virtually everything that a support person can do. In larger firms that do a greater volume of business, the job will be more narrowly described, but in both cases there will be some constants.

1. You will participate in client interviews.
2. You will meet with clients to complete petitions and schedules.
3. You will be assigned the drafting of routine motions, filing and organizing of case files, and preparing of a "tickler system" and/or docketing schedule.
4. You will be on the phone quite a bit with creditors and you will take trips to the court to attend hearings and file petitions.

There is a personal component that should not be overlooked. Strong emotions surround this experience for your clients, so you must be a calm force in the middle of a hurricane of tension, questions, and a deep desire to just "get all this done and finished." Master the filing deadlines and U.S. Bankruptcy Rules. It also does not hurt to befriend the court clerks at the U.S. Bankruptcy Court in your area. Your attorney will rely upon you to be on top of the cases with which you are entrusted. You should be able to give a quick report to the attorney asking about the status of a case.

## Working for the creditor

Paralegals who work for creditors are working for clients who are business concerns, banks, or other such entities. Larger firms often have such clients, and thus the bankruptcy work sometimes naturally falls to them. This work usually involves Chapter 11's more than Chapter 7's. There is a greater emphasis therefore on cases with hundreds and even thousands of documents involving the potential demise of a business or corporation. Document control, computer and wordprocessing skills, and big-case management come into play. In fact, the work differs vastly for a creditor- and a debtor-orientation, yet you are dealing with the same court and rules.

With creditor bankruptcy law you will:

1) file documents and prepare motions
2) review case files and motions and be the "fact expert" on those cases (There are lots of numbers and calculations in this area; be ready for numbers.)
3) do docketing, attend hearings
4) review court files

## Working for the Chapter 7 trustee

A woman who works for a Chapter 7 trustee exclaims that she enjoys the work because she "meets all the players" and gets to know lots of people. She works on a database for the bankruptcy system. She feels as if she is in the very middle of the process and enjoys bringing things to a resolution. This paralegal job requires staying on top of other people's business. "There is a relief," she says, "in not worrying about whether everything is correct before filing, and there is a sense of control in working for the trustee."

## The Real Estate Paralegal

This kind of paralegal works with fixed forms and among the many moving parts of the world of real estate law. This world can encompass foreclosures, closings, quiet title actions, and the realm of title companies. (By the way, title companies are hiring more and more paralegals because of their excellent awareness of the basic issues involved. Pay is increasing in some areas of the country and paralegals are being promoted up into management at title companies.)

### The closing

The main tension-producing moment in this practice area is the closing. It is a moment in time at which everyone concerned must be in attendance, everyone in attendance must be of complete agreement, and everyone in attendance must have documents that agree with everyone else's. It is the climax of agreement coming from parties who may have been at odds with each other for days (or weeks or months).

The real estate paralegal has to have an eye for detail and an ability to bring comprehension, consistency, and accuracy to literally hundreds of documents. This process can be both dreaded and addictive. Understand that real estate class can in no way imitate what the closing is. One woman who owns a successful agency marketing temporary paralegals to a large metropolitan area once declared,

> Never say you'll never go into a certain practice area. Keep your options open. I swore I would never go into Real Estate based upon my classroom experience. Five years later, I had five years of experience in Real Estate. I became addicted to that practice area.

Your firm may represent the buyer or the seller in a closing, and might also represent the borrower/lender. The documents, checklists, and preclosing steps differ depending on whom you are helping. The process is a constant interrelating of all the parties involved. Contracts must be drafted, as well as addendums and counterproposals, and all the while each must coordinate with the other to be sure there is agreement. Title work will have to be done while you are ordering special coverages and a tax certificate. There will be a surveyor, who may have changes and corrections on his work. Loan pay-off documents must be prepared, assumable loans and new loans will all have to have the proper documentation, and leases must be reviewed and checked in case they might affect the closing. And all the while, you must be taking care that any documents that are not viable do not get mixed up with the new corrected versions. It always falls to the paralegal to double- and triple-check that all the documents are current and correct.

Work toward the closing must be done with one eye toward complete accuracy and the other on the clock. Inaccuracy can kill a closing, but mostly it can cost *time*, which is crucial at closings. Check the Deeds and Bill of Sale and all the pertinent loan documents. Remember you will be obtaining the canceled notes, releases, and new title policies. And don't forget those originals. With just a brief snapshot of what goes on at a closing, you can see the "adrenaline rush" that participants enjoy as they mount their efforts and watch something come to a resolved conclusion.

If you are working with a bank as borrower, you will be involved with corporate law too. There will be U.C.C. searches, certificates of good standing for corporations or certificates of registration for limited partnerships. There will be lien waivers and certificates of completion if a construction project is involved. There will be zoning questions and ordinances to be followed. In these situations paralegals are relied upon for the initial acquisition and verification of many of these documents. They must be thorough and have great amounts of what many applicants call "follow through."

Real estate paralegals must know the step-by-step procedure for completing successful foreclosures and judicial foreclosures and be prepared to bring their special expertise to many practice areas that they might not anticipate. If one files for bankruptcy, real estate is almost always affected. Corporate law is often involved in real estate transactions, and since the *land* is what we are talking about here, probate law looms large in real estate practice, as old generations transfer power and wealth to new generations. Litigation often involves real estate because it is one of the world's chief forms of wealth.

## The Traditional Setting Still Employs Seven Out of Ten Paralegals

This fact should tell us that there are lots of different paralegals out there in law firms who do not fall under Litigation, Real Estate, and Bankruptcy practice areas. These were chosen simply to paint a picture of complex activity done by thoroughly qualified and fully occupied professional paralegals. Thousands of paralegals work under various practice area specialty names.

Perhaps the first one, which in many ways is more challenging than any other, is the *general practice*. This means that you must be prepared to study up on areas you have not handled before. Once these specialty areas are fully absorbed into the conscious and subconscious they can get much easier than they might first appear, but the generalist paralegal "hath a continual challenge": facing what comes through the door next. Most general practice areas are simply short ways of saying, "We handle about five practice areas, plus, Mr. Client, if you get a D.U.I., we will represent you."

There are also numerous other practice areas:

Antitrust Paralegals
Domestic Paralegals
Bilingual Generalist Paralegals
Workers' Comp Paralegals
Personal Injury Paralegals
Insurance Defense Paralegals
Water Law Paralegals
Immigration and Naturalization Paralegals
Entertainment Law Paralegals
Civil Rights Paralegals
Employment Law Paralegals
Environmental Paralegals
Product Liability Paralegals
Lender Liability Paralegals
Securities Paralegals
Corporate Paralegals
Criminal Paralegals
Commercial Paralegals

The list goes on. If there is an area of law, there can be a paralegal attached to that area who is deeply involved to the full occupation of that paralegal's time. Paralegals practice in several areas over a period of time and do tend toward specialization as opportunity pushes one toward one practice or another. While you are developing a breadth of practice area experience in your progress from entry-level status, various chances to focus on a specialty area will most likely present themselves to you. The beauty of the paralegal world is that you are never completely pigeon-holed unless you desire to focus in on a special practice area. Whether by choice or circumstance a specialty can gain you more pay, a sense of authority, and a higher perceived value among your peers and coworkers. The best pay in the largest cities goes to the paralegals who are virtual "authorities" in their practice area.

An overall career formula . . .
. . . may be to get wide experience as you begin and also work toward a specialty as opportunities arise.

## In-House Counsel

A new association is rising up to represent a growing number of paralegals who populate the halls of Corporate America. Corporations must have counsel, and small companies may have an attorney on retainer. In this situation, the paralegal deals with the company as a client and bills time. As companies grow, they continue this relationship with an attorney or switch to a larger law firm that can provide a full array of services. There may be a team of paralegals and attorneys that handle the XYZ corporation's legal matters: employment law matters, intellectual property matters, contract and vendor matters, and corporate matters.

Eventually the company sees a real need to hire an attorney to work with both the officers and executives and deal with outside counsel. Sometimes the in-house counsel office remains small—the attorney has a secretary and maybe a paralegal. The meetings (small matters of representation and corporate activities) stay in-house, and then larger litigated or complex matters go to the outside counsel. This is the point where many companies are, in terms of their legal support. The inside attorney, a full-time employee of the corporation, and sometimes a vice president handle all legal matters and then determine what goes outside.

### Corporate counsel legal assistants

It really does not matter what service the company performs or product it makes: you, as a paralegal, could be working for a company in any state that has hired an attorney who is full-time, in-house corporate counsel. As these positions become more and more numerous, the quality of paralegal work in this area increasingly attains its own identity. Corporate law, employment law, intellectual property, and other matters increasingly fall to in-house support. A paralegal who works for an interstate gas company says she loves the job because of the "predictable variety and the travel." She says, "I travel just enough to keep things interesting, but not so much that it gets tedious." Corporate counsel paralegals are a growing army out there; and with a national association (the American Corporate Legal Assistants Association), the use of paralegals in this area will grow even more and benefit from the identity that the association creates.

## Why is paralegal work in the corporate world growing?

More and more accountants and executives in corporate America are concluding that they can hire attorneys and paralegals as employees. From a career point of view, a paralegal has an opportunity to be a corporate employee, getting benefits and the chance to be promoted within the corporation. The trend toward larger in-house counsel staffs (bringing in greater numbers of legal support to handle large litigation matters) means that the paralegal will become even more viable. That viability will increase because the billing system of the firm is not in force. If a paralegal can do a job and is trained for it, the paralegal will probably be given the responsibility, in view of the fact that the paralegal will still be supervised by in-house counsel. There will not be an economic incentive to give the work to the attorney.

A few specific growth areas are also contributing to the growth of paralegal employment within corporations.

### Growth in Insurance

A large and successful national insurance company is building an addition onto one of their regional headquarters. Why? Their litigation department will be housed there. Insurance companies across the country are concluding that instead of "farming out" their litigation matters to large firms, they can hire a firm, make them full-time employees, and keep them busy. The insurance company would no longer scrutinize large bills with hourly fees; it cuts paychecks to attorneys and paralegals who are their own employees.

In addition, trained paralegals are applying for and getting positions with titles like "policy service representative," for which they are being trained for several months. One paralegal exclaimed to me, "I am having to learn about the insurance laws for seven different states in our region. And after that, I have to be ready to train our agents concerning their policies in all these different states!" Insurance is a field that promises great growth for people trained as paralegals. The paralegal status will continue to benefit them all the way through the promotions in their career as insurance professionals.

### Corporations That Provide Legal Services

As computerized litigation support grows more complex, many firms have gone into the business of serving government agencies and large corporations with special expertise. The Environmental Protection Agency, for example, hires subcontracting companies to assist them in the determination of "potentially responsible parties." Consulting agencies serve the "potentially responsible parties," which are usually large companies.

Paralegals who work in these companies work with database management systems and employ experience gained in practices like research and real estate. There is also a strong technical/scientific component to the work involved. People with science majors and experience that do not at first appear to be transferrable to the legal world could have backgrounds that fit in with fields like "environmental." From toxic waste disposal, to chemical analysis, to the measurement of "ambient air particles," the broad term "environmental" encompasses many technical and scientific disciplines.

## Government

Paralegals work in federal agencies, state agencies, and municipal and county offices. They work for judges and court administrators throughout the state court systems. A paralegal in an office of a state attorney general says, "We have paralegals working throughout the offices of the state attorney general. Since we are the legal counsel for the state, we have our hands on numerous projects continually. From consumer fraud to working with the corrections system, paralegals are there providing the necessary support."

Paralegals work as investigators for subcontractors who are paid by federal agencies. Are they federal employees? Not really. And that is the reason that there is work at every level of government. Working for the government worker means that sometimes you are an employee of a subcontractor of an agency. So, under the broad category of "government" we must also include again, "corporations."

## Trends in Paralegal Employment Areas

Increased regulation by federal, state, and local agencies, the corresponding need for compliance and legal responses to these regulations, the continued rise of litigation as a remedy to conflict, consumerism, activism, and social evolution are all leading to increased legal activity. These trends tend to benefit the paralegal. The legal profession will continue to grow in different ways and attorneys will always have work to do. The questions lie in how firms will fare and how legal services will be delivered to the consumer. And yet with all of these developments, there remains a basic vital truth: the trained and skilled paralegal has a future inside law firms, corporations, government, and other diverse settings. You, as a flexible and imaginative job hunter, have a much bigger world out there than you might imagine. The person who only looks under "L" (for Legal Assistant) and "P" (for Paralegal) is missing a host of "legal positions" out there for which they would be qualified to apply—if they only knew they were named "contract specialist" or "vendor administrator" or "policy service representative."

# CHAPTER 3

---

## *Winning Job Search Strategies*
### *"First Moves" That Lead to Job Offers*

Effective job strategies and "first moves" that get attention are invaluable for some very obvious reasons. It helps to rehearse, though, because looking for a job is the most difficult and arduous task most people can imagine. Public speaking is said to be number one on most individuals' "fear list," and being unemployed is most likely number one on their "dread list." (And public speaking *during* a job search in an interview combines fear and dread.) Losing your job and being unemployed is the thing that most people truly *fear* as a possibility. Other fears may be visceral and subconscious or may be about sudden physical calamity. But the fear that lives with the populace on a daily level is the one surrounding the issue of employment.

Seen in a more positive light, we can say that humans are made to be busy. As a species, we want to be engaged in some enterprise. Americans tend to define themselves by what they *do*. Besides answering survival needs and financing American culture's wonderful amenities, getting work of any kind often makes the difference between self-respect and feeling lost. In fact, many paralegals choose part-time or temporary legal employment while they are looking for that "ideal" full-time legal position simply because having a job gives security and experience. Finding employment is plainly our most significant response to the challenge of living, and working "in the paralegal field" gives the worker identity, meaning, and momentum.

## The Paralegal Job Hunter: Employed vs. Unemployed

The unemployed paralegal job hunter's task is challenging. The professional effort of looking for openings, writing letters, and interviewing is taxing, and the need to be poised and at your best while being unemployed is a constant requirement. In effect, you must be at your best when you really feel at your worst.

Have you ever looked for a job when you had a job? It is a completely different experience. As an employed job hunter, you may not feel fulfilled or you may fear impending unemployment, but you interview with security; you hold yourself with confidence. The expression "relaxed, but alert" really means something to you. Try to look for a job when you have a job. It is a wholly different experience.

But those who are entry level in any profession must start at the beginning. The entry paralegal must start at the *entry-level hump*. This is the most difficult part of your career. And you face it in the very beginning, for it is now that you must look your best, feel your best, interview your best, and *be* at your best, overall. Yet it is now that we do not have work and are wondering how to pay our bills. Every night our fears tuck us into bed as our hopes shoo them away and make plans for tomorrow.

Job hunters without employment—and that is how we will think of job hunters in this book—face a daily challenge to be effective. They must marry their ambition and positive attitudes to effective strategies that work and to plans that are designed for an extended job search. People who can do this will begin with effective first moves, because they have a whole array of activity to bring to the job search playing field.

## Full-Time Temp

You must think of yourself as *employed* when you are looking for a job. You are, in effect, working for yourself. When you look for a job, your employer is you, your paymaster is the future, and your profession is "effective job seeker." In reality, if you are doing it right, you are anything but *unemployed* when you are "unemployed." If you view this task as an occasional expenditure of your life's energies, your job search will be difficult indeed. Do not view your job as an effective job searcher as that of a "part-time temp"; you will not create enough activity. Do not view your job as a permanent position; that points to days in the unemployment line as your life's work. See yourself as a "full-time temp." Armed with strategies and plans for an all-out effort, you should be an effective job seeker.

Many job hunters approach the challenge of finding a job with the correct attitudes and a persistent determination to succeed in that role. But why don't we just admit going in that it is the most taxing of all jobs — the job of getting a job is the toughest job. Merely facing that fact with a positive attitude will give you power.

What can we learn from the job hunters who are doing it right? They are *working*. They have the right *philosophies* and the right *information*. They don't look at unemployment statistics or let negative fears slow them down.

The paralegal job hunter is aided by the growth this profession is predicted to continue enjoying, but is challenged by the increased competition of viable applicants. Being educated in a profession as you have been is not enough to gain the entrance you seek to this professional world. There are areas of *knowledge* and *philosophy* that are important for each paralegal job seeker to know.

As a professional paralegal job hunter, you must have the "look and feel" of a potential employee; you must approach the prospective employer with the right language and the right image, speaking the necessary meaningful "buzz words." The more you look like the professional that they are envisioning, the less likely it is you will suffer early disqualification. But before we talk about effort, good luck, bad luck, timing, and "striking while the iron is hot," we must address just who you are as a future paralegal.

## The Profession Filled with "Transitionals"

Because the world of law is as diverse as society itself and therefore can utilize many kinds of past experiences, the paralegal profession embraces generalists and potpourri backgrounds. This cuts both ways. The paralegal profession is filled with people with past employment experiences, knowing different interview protocols, different rules for resumes, and different expectations of the job hunt in general. Paralegal graduates need to think about how the legal job search differs from their past experience. Those new paralegals who are simply young probably need to educate themselves about the professional job hunt itself. In either case, both groups must prepare to mount a proper job hunt based upon the professional world they are attempting *to enter*, not the one they *just left*.

Many people are rejected for reasons that would amaze them. Many rejections occur because of a lack of sophistication and understanding, not because they are unqualified or make a negative impression. We all have our particular pride. Some say: "I am a great natural interviewer." Others say: "I do not need lessons on how to write a cover letter." Still others say: "Just give me the paralegal certificate. I've been writing resumes for ten years, and I just spent $75.00 on this one."

Sometimes we do not equate our transition with our need to develop skills to persuade people that we can be a valuable employee. You are transitioning to a new career, and your job search skills also need transitioning. It is as if we declare: "All right, I'll admit I need a special education to *prepare* for this new world, but I won't admit I need special training to *enter* this new world."

One troubled job hunter asked me, after several interviews had ended with no offers, why she was not getting into the second or third interview stage. I had her rehearse her "bio" (personal story, education, skills, and benefits) to me. When she covered her past 15 years she talked about her life as an administrator. She emphasized her supervisory skills, her hiring and firing of personnel, and her ability to direct the working lives of 20 other people. I asked her, "Did it not take tremendous organizational ability, a persuasive personality, and a dedicated work ethic to attain that level of responsibility?" She replied in the affirmative. **"Then stop emphasizing your *titles* and start emphasizing your *skills*." This is one of the biggest mistakes people make in search of paralegal employment.** They forget that entry paralegals will most likely *not* be hiring and firing, directing other people, and performing duties related to the personnel department. People make these mistakes simply because they have not thought long enough about the *differences* between the legal world they are hoping to enter and the world they have just left.

## Elements of the Job Hunt

Your particular stage in life is not as important as your awareness of the need to use the right vocabulary and have the right approach in the legal job search process. In addition to all the techniques and approaches that are particular to the legal job hunt (which will be discussed in greater detail in the following chapters), there are the invigorating challenges of the job hunt itself. It is in our *first moves* that the job hunt's success can be foreseen. No matter who you are or where you come from, you must fit into a broad, general category of **employable paralegal candidate**. A well-placed and effective effort using tried and true first moves and strategies can be very persuasive.

Now let us address those things that affect the "well-placed and effective effort." The following elements can affect your job hunt:

- good fortune and bad fortune
- number of contacts
- you only need one job
- you never know what contact will lead to a job

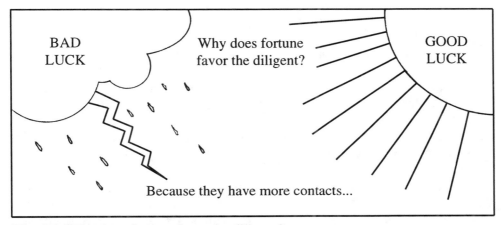

**Fig. 3-1** Why does fortune favor the diligent?

## *Good fortune and bad fortune*

What is it that makes life exciting but at the same time tough to comprehend? It is the presence and mixture of both good and bad fortune. When three people have interviewed well, have conducted professional job searches, and are waiting on a Friday afternoon for a phone call, they are all subject to the fortune/misfortune factor. Assuming they all performed equally well, the hiring decision will probably be highly subjective and based upon the subtext of interview drama. It is 4:00 in the afternoon: One receives an offer over the phone. Two get letters in the mail. Fortune/misfortune has determined the outcome.

The natural reaction for the rejected pair is to blame themselves. In fact, there may be no blame to be placed. In the world of the job search, we seem to be only observers. The narcotic of blame and reaction and fatalism *feeds* off the process that we call the fortune/misfortune factor.

And yet there is a very *positive* way to deal with this aspect of the paralegal job search.

Who does not want good fortune? Americans are crazy about lotteries for a basic human reason: A part of us, however small and unconscious it might be, wishes for a sudden external act to lift us high above our daily life. When we are looking for a job, that seed can flower into a full-blown shade tree. The job search and our personal situation blend together to make us wish for an external entity to magically solve all our problems!

> There is a formula
> For Minimizing Bad Fortune
> And Maximizing Good Fortune
> But . . .
> It involves Work.

Assume for a moment that we are all subject to good fortune and bad fortune at the same rate. (It may not be true, but the truth will not be revealed to everyone's satisfaction in the near future.) If fortune/misfortune occur at a rate that is the same for all of us, then it is easy to see why those who do less are more dependent on fortune. They are counting on the same good results as one who is diligently working overtime at job hunting. It is also easy to see why hard-working, driven job seekers say things like, "People make their own luck." If fortune occurs at the same rate, then in a way we *do* make our own luck. Other elements of the job search can help you make some of that luck.

## 200 contacts vs. 25 contacts

Any seminar in insurance sales will tell you that sales success is a matter of simple arithmetic. The phrase you hear in these seminars is, "It's a numbers game." This attempt to reduce the problem to a matter of arithmetic is designed to focus the salespeople on keeping up their numbers of contacts. If they spend too much time on old contacts that show little promise, they are not playing the sales game correctly. In the effective job search, the challenge is much the same.

If you make 200 contacts (or 25 contacts) over a given time, you will experience good fortune and bad fortune in a certain proportion. Of course, you disregard the bad fortune and maximize the good fortune. The one with 200 contacts has "more" good luck—more chances for good fortune to play a role—and so can play the opportunities against themselves and take more control of the negotiating process. The one who has made only 25 contacts over the same period of time is going to react more strongly to the bad fortune, and will "hope and pray" that the good fortune brings employment, thus minimizing negotiating power and confidence. This process is like a roulette wheel to the latter, more like a card game to the former.

Let's look back at our three job seekers from page 35. Job Seeker #1, Anne, got the job offer. The next week she would get calls from two other people for interviews because her job search was active enough that she had "several arrows in the air" at once. Her "crop was coming in" and she was reaping.

Job Seeker #2, David, suffered a "downturn" for a time after his rejection because he was counting on getting that job. He was counting too much on one event. He stopped all activity on his job hunt while the interview process was taking place. He had a "special feeling" about that job from the first time he saw it advertised. The first interviewer made him feel so good that he was sure the offer was 80 percent complete. He was devastated when he was turned down. Since he had ceased all other activity, his sadness slipped into depression. It took him ten days to get back in a proper job hunting frame of mind, and then because he had not been making contacts there was less "crop coming in" as the weeks passed.

Job Seeker #3, Marjorie, was disappointed that she was turned down. She went home that night, talked it over with her husband and went to see a movie to get through the negative feelings. By Sunday, she had her nose back in the newspapers and was conducting a direct mail campaign for a practice area in which she was interested. But this was nothing new; she had been conducting a fruitful search ever since her graduation. The next week, she got two interviews from mailings and contacts she had made a month before. She had too much momentum to slow down. She was too busy making things happen to go into a two-week funk.

### Remember: you only need one job

One key element separates job hunting from sales. In sales, you must perform and succeed and meet quotas every month. **In job hunting, you just need that one job. Once you get that one full-time paralegal job, your job search can go on "hold."** After an arduous job search, I once received two offers in one day. When the jubilation died down I stared blankly into the TV and listened to my wife's gentle admonition: "You can't show up at both jobs. You have to accept just one of them."

She startled me out of my partial paralysis on the evening I had to decide between two offers. This is the heartening, but ironic, twist to this process, if you are lucky enough to entertain multiple offers.

One graduate mailed 92 letters to her home state of Nebraska. Some went to Omaha, some to Lincoln. She also mailed letters and resumes to advertised leads. About three weeks after graduation, she was entertaining three offers in a three-day period. Two were in Omaha and one in Lincoln. She decided to turn down the Lincoln offer because it was just a little lower than the one in Omaha. On the day she was leaving her apartment (she was staying in Lincoln at the time), the Lincoln firm called her up and said, "We are not going to let you get away from us. How about $2,000 more per year?" This example demonstrates that one piece of good fortune can play off another. She was able to maximize all of her good fortune and end up with a pleasing result. But, in the end, she could only take one of those jobs.

## *Which contact will lead to a job?*

Maximum effort is necessary because you never know what is going to work! Ask the woman in Lincoln about the original 92 letters she sent out. Ask her if 75 would have worked, or just 20. She cannot know. Efficiency cannot be a goal in the job search. Only *after* the fact can you see what worked and what did not work. The only thing you can do is work your hardest. **You never know what contact will lead to that one job you need.** If you are half-hearted in your effort, you will always wonder how much more effort might have worked. Effort is the pure and simple answer to the fortune/misfortune factor. Work hard, so then you can feel secure and poised to take advantage of the results.

Before we go into detailing effective job search strategies, let's review the necessary first moves:

1. Looking for a job is an emotionally grueling and psychologically demanding experience.
2. But employment is worth the effort. We define ourselves by what we do. Employment is not only a necessity, it is our first and largest response to the challenge of living.
3. The job hunt finds you at your worst when you need to be at your best.
4. Since full-time work is what you need, turn finding a job into a job. See yourself as an employed "Full-Time Temp," with the goal of being an effective paralegal job seeker.
5. Strategies and plans that work in the legal profession over the long-term are essential to this full-time temp job.
6. The paralegal profession is growing and provides constant new opportunities for the candidate.
7. The effective paralegal job seeker must have a level of sophistication and understanding to be considered a viable, employable

paralegal candidate. You must look, act, and sound like an employable paralegal.

8. Though fortune and misfortune are real factors in the job hunt, more effort and increased contacts maximize good fortune and decrease the significance of bad fortune.

9. You need only *one job*. You must work as hard as you can on your job search, because you never know what contact will lead to that one job you need.

10. The effective paralegal job seeker needs strategies.

## Strategies for Approaching Law Firms of Different Sizes

### The sole practitioner

Do not think of a sole practitioner as a "country lawyer." Avoid assumptions about where the attorney comes from or whether the practice has the "sophistication" of a large firm. It is best to meet sole practitioners as you find them and respond to their stated needs. A sole practitioner might have left a large firm because of a desire for independence and being one's own boss. He or she might have been practicing for the last 30 years and have a client list inherited from a multi-generation law family, or might want to:

1) remain a sole practitioner for his or her entire career;
2) grow to a certain small controllable level, take on several partners, and then stop there;
3) become the biggest law firm in the city and eventually hold the position of senior partner in that firm;
4) reestablish himself or herself after a firm break-up and eventually grow back to a larger size.

While you cannot assume certain things about this kind of attorney, you can still make some very solid assumptions based simply upon the fact that they are alone and have a relatively small number of support personnel:

♦ The sole practitioner will want support personnel to wear more than one hat.
♦ The sole practitioner will probably want you to work with clients to a certain degree.

♦ The sole practitioner will need wordprocessing support.
♦ The sole practitioner will hire based upon an array of priorities.

*"Find a Need and Fill It."*
Common Entrepreneurial Saying

This much-quoted saying speaks volumes when it comes to approaching a sole practitioner. When I take job orders for entry paralegals from sole practitioners, the conversation typically goes like this.

| | |
|---|---|
| *Sole Practitioner:* | I need someone to help me out with my practice. You know . . . someone who can help me out in every area. I need someone who is willing to answer the phone, handle document preparation, do client interviews, help me with billing, make filings at court—things a paralegal can do. You know, do everything which I normally do when I can't do it. Do you have anybody like that? |
| *Career Development:* | Certainly! What's your practice area? |
| *SP:* | I handle almost everything that comes through the door, but mainly my practice is personal injury, Workers' Comp, criminal defense, some real estate, some estate planning, and some family law. I need someone who can train quickly, who's bright and enthusiastic, can handle the computer, be good with people, and work hard. |

### Many a Paralegal Career Started with a Sole Practitioner

Every employment situation has positives and negatives. You will hear paralegals argue until they are blue in the face as to why they hate real estate and love litigation and vice versa. You can hear a horror story about a sole practitioner, and then turn around and hear one about a large law firm. Despite all of the comparing and complaining, the one key point that may get overlooked is: In the quest for that hard to find *first* paralegal job, sole practitioners are more flexible and are more likely to give entry paralegals an opportunity if they like the way the applicant interviews and if his or her training and background meet their needs.

The sole practitioner does not have to check with a hiring partner, "run you by" a special committee, or worry about whether the senior partner is going to like you. The sole practitioner *is* the hiring partner, the committee, the senior partner, and every other management/legal title there is. He or she can pick you because you seem to be the best choice out of all those who have interviewed for the position. Many a paralegal career had its beginning in the hunch of a sole practitioner who thought that a certain someone would be just right for their practice and clientele.

### What Does the Sole Practitioner Need?

Strategies that work with sole practitioners are ones that demonstrate an understanding of their particular world. The world of the sole practitioner is different from the lawyer in the large firm. Same profession, different lives. The sole practitioner must worry about the business end of the practice, so the more accounting, balancing, bookkeeping, and/or cash handling you have done the more practical and "real world" you will appear. The sole practitioner needs clients coming through the door, and values people who have had exposure to the public or been in customer service situations. A background in which you have learned that "the customer is always right" actually has meaning to a sole practitioner. Although you will not be relied upon to get clients or keep them, the sole practitioner is often concerned that clients will be impressed with your professionalism, appearance, and conduct. In some practices, the main support paralegal has close and continual contact with many key clients, in contrast to a large law firm where client contact is often minimal. (When paralegals in large firms are given client contact responsibilities, it is a sign of great trust. We will get to large firm issues later in this chapter.)

Successful sole practitioners have probably stood at the copy machine until midnight once or twice. They expect the same flexibility from you. Sole practitioners often make their own coffee and prepare their own documents. They have purchased their own equipment, or leased it. The sole practitioner does not see work separated out like a union shop in which certain individuals will not do this and others can only do that; he or she sees an end result—getting work out the door and keeping clients content. Work is what *everyone* pushes out the door. **A sole practitioner knows how to interview for the quality of *flexibility*. They will ask "what if" questions and hypotheticals to determine what kind of worker you will be.** Expect questions such as:

- ◆ What do you consider your most important attribute as an employee?
- ◆ Are you willing to make filings in court occasionally or run an errand or two?

◆ You probably have some favorite practice areas. How would you feel about working in a general practice like mine?

If you exude the qualities of enthusiasm, flexibility, energy, and "roll your sleeves up" gusto, then you will outmaneuver paralegals who go to their interviews touting their high marks in legal research class.

### Approach: Friendly and Personal, Even (If You Dare) in Person

In general, you will find handing out resumes in person from office to office walking down Main Street to be an unsuccessful and discouraging exercise. You get so few interviews for all of your effort. Applicants with resumes are generally stopped at the front desk by the receptionist. However, it *might* work with the sole practitioner.

Approaching a sole practitioner on your feet with a cover letter and resume in hand takes a degree of boldness that most do not have, and it may seem to be a nonproductive use of time. In many cases it is. But because the sole practitioner is often in a small office, is more accessible, and is often more egalitarian and less stuffy than his or her big firm counterpart, showing up in person with a resume and a cover letter properly addressed *could* get you an interview.

If the sole practitioner is not around or cannot be made available to you, be very warm to the person who takes your letter and resume. Do not push. This is the very reason you must have a cover letter prepared ahead of time. If you do not get an audience, you have a letter that explains your purpose. By simply dropping off a resume without a cover letter, you are signaling that you are unprepared and you are just "trying your luck" blitzing a certain part of the city. If you succeed at having a chat with a sole practitioner who just might greet you at the door or give you a casual interview, then you have reached a decision maker—someone who can hire you!

One paralegal candidate discovered that if she called between 5:00 and 5:30 in the afternoon, the attorney would answer the phone. She concluded that a visit might have a good result. She walked into a law office in a small shopping center at 5:15 one day and struck up a conversation with the only person there—the sole practitioner herself, sitting at the front desk, writing a note. She got a short friendly interview that led to an offer three weeks later.

### Wordprocessing and the Sole Practitioner: "Can You Type?"

Today's paralegal *must* have a reasonable typing speed and be willing to learn any software programs to which they are exposed. If you obtain employment that does not require much wordprocessing and computer utilization, get ready, because your next job will. That being said, if you are writing to, speaking with, and networking amongst sole practitioners, be sure that they are going to want you to fit into their computer and wordprocessing needs. Sole practitioners will hire people who fit into their situations with enthusiasm, skill, and versatility.

When I obtained my first entry-level employment in 1985, a sole practitioner looked me over at an interview in a cafe. The attorney looked over his steaming cup of coffee and out the window as he asked, "Can you type?" I assured him that I could, since I had done some editing and writing in a past profession. I also assured him that I did not mind typing and that I could get the work out that needed to get out—and that I would stay late to get it out.

Wordprocessing and computer proficiency is demanded of paralegals at every level nowadays, but for sole practitioners it is *an absolute requirement*. This does *not* mean you will be typing all day. The strategy you must employ with a sole practitioner is to convey an attitude of confidence, ease, and comfort with wordprocessing. Usually, they do not want to train you; they want the technical aspect of the practice to be a "given" going in.

They are concerned about it because they do not want to have to worry about it. Sole practitioner #1 might have no other support personnel besides you. This means you will be responsible for all the wordprocessing apart from that which the attorney produces. Sole practitioner #2, however, might have a secretary and an associate. In this situation, you might be responsible for occasional secretarial work, your own work, and pleadings preparation. Let's look at how that might happen in a hypothetical office with a sole practitioner, an associate, and one secretary:

1) Fill in for the secretary on sick days, vacation days, and lunch hours, and be capable of handling everything that the secretary does. Answer the phone, deal with clients, and handle notices and communications with opposing counsel.
2) Always be able to perform all of your own assignments so that the secretary is not burdened with an additional workload. Remember, if you are a burden to the already overworked secretary, then the sole practitioner does not benefit from hiring you.
3) Volunteer to handle the docketing if they do not ask you to first. This will relieve the secretary, give you an automatic view of the entire case load, and make you immediately valuable.

Remember, sole practitioners tend to focus on your technical abilities so that when filing deadlines are looming and late afternoon hours approach, they know that everyone will contribute. **The message is simple:** *Do not let a lack of computer skills be an obstacle to your hiring.*

## Summary: advantages and disadvantages of working with a sole practitioner

1) Advantages
   a) Greater consideration is given to the individual applicant than to the level of experience. A sole practitioner may be more likely to hire an entry person.
   b) You can learn about how a law practice works: The ins and outs, the filings, the rules for service and evidence, and the many complex details that make a law office function. These fundamentals are invaluable.
   c) If personalities are well matched and the working atmosphere is reasonable, it can be a full, varied, and enjoyable experience. With the right chemistry, this can be the most fun and rewarding experience for a paralegal.
2) Disadvantages
   a) The pay can be lower than in small, medium, or large firms. Many sole practitioners realize that they are giving you an entrée into the profession and thus feel that this is a trade-off for the beginning paralegal.
   b) If you want a calm and ordered work setting, a sole practitioner's practice can be a difficult place to work. His or her practice will be filled with change and unpredictability on a daily basis.
   c) Because of the intimate setting, working with a sole practitioner can be extremely uncomfortable if there is bad chemistry. Your sole practitioner may be working alone for a reason. Since you must see each other *every day*, if you do not like each other as people (or at least respect each other) you can be in for a long and wearing tour of duty—or a short one.

### Strategy for Winning Over a Sole Practitioner

Let us assume you have made contact, you have the proper qualifications, and you are being considered along with other candidates. The winning candidate will probably be (all other factors being relatively equal) the one who builds *enthusiasm* in the sole practitioner about his or her practice and the role of the paralegal in it. You must:

1) Be persuasive and convincing about your flexibility and enthusiasm.
2) Ask questions about the practice. Build a level of genuine interest in the sole practitioner's practice areas. Convey your excitement for this new profession. Generate a sense of team spirit. Remember, the sole practitioner is succeeding without a full team of cohorts and equals; what little team they have is very important to them.

Looking like an enthusiastic potential team member and exhibiting flexibility are attractive features to any size law firm, but the sole practitioner has a personal attachment to their practice unlike members of larger firms. The key attraction then is not only your skills and enthusiasm but, most significantly, your ability to communicate a strongly felt desire to work for that person as a professional.

## Small and midsize firms

Strategies for appealing to small and midsize firms vary according to practice area and the firms' internal organizational structure. From the first contact to the last interview, the challenge for the aspiring paralegal is to be informed about the law firm, so let's look at the internal organizational structure of these firms.

They usually have four to ten attorneys (the partner/associate ratio varies), and a legal administrator, office manager, business manager and/or a combination person who handles these assignments or farms them out. There are secretaries and paralegals and maybe a part-time runner/file clerk.

How does this firm approach hiring? There comes a point in the evolution of a law firm when a person making *paralegal hiring decisions* is appointed. At some partnership meeting in which one partner was attempting to hire a friend of a friend, and another was interviewing someone she met at a professional luncheon, they all concluded that the hiring of support personnel should be under one person. There are different ways to handle this process, but a common one is to have a hiring partner work with an office manager. The hiring partner may change yearly or less often, but the office manager does much of the preliminary screening and early interviewing. Often it falls to the office manager to do the initial interviewing of the paralegals, with the recruiting and advertising for associates being assigned to an attorney.

### Who Is the Contact Person?

A common strategy that often misfires is to just write to the *first named partner in the firm.* A quick look at the Martindale-Hubbell directory of lawyers may reveal that he is dead, or Of Counsel, or so old that you know he does not interview paralegals, or (more likely than anything else) just does not have the time to interview paralegals, especially the first time around.

Many do not even take that quick look at a resource book. They simply call the firm and ask something like "Who would I *write to* regarding the hiring of paralegals?" or "I need the name of the person in the firm who would receive paralegal resumes." They may be given an associate's name, a junior partner's name, a senior partner's name, or an office manager's or business manager's name, depending upon the size of the firm and their philosophy about paralegals. *They may not be given the right name.* Without the proper contact name, their letters could be immediately tossed into the wastebasket by the first person who opens them.

### Usefulness of Networking

The topic of *networking* will be discussed throughout this book, but at this point I've introduced it to show you how to approach the small and midsize firm when you have a *networking contact.* A networking contact is someone who knows a working attorney through any source, other than an advertisement. With this contact, written or oral communication on your part can lead to interviews. Networking is the key to employment.

You must also be aware of (and wary of) firm politics when you interact with your friend or contact. A barrier or labyrinth exists at the front door of a law office. The back door, or the path of networking, does not have the same barricade to the decision makers. Often, due to networking, you are talking to decision makers very early in the process. Below, we will discuss some of the advantages, and pitfalls, of networking within a small or midsize firm.

### Honor the Organizational Structure of the Firm

If networking is the source of *jobs that are hard to find, but easier to get,* then **part of the work you must do when you network is to learn the political terrain of the firm and understand its organizational structure as you begin networking.**

Suppose you have interviewed with a young partner at a small firm. She seems to like you and wants you to interview with others. You may have an ally in this partner, *but you still have to go through the formal interview process.* It would be quite helpful to write to the legal administrator/office manager early on in the process, so that if the partner mentions your name in a meeting or in passing the administrator will know who you are. Simply be ready to walk through each step of the process, mindful that each person with whom you speak has an important role to play in your hiring. Many people have used a networking contact profitably and then interviewed with an "administrator" who disqualified them. Often it is because proper "respect" for the administrator was not shown in the process. When a person is given charge of the hiring process, it is all-important for you — the approaching applicant — to address that interview with as much consideration as you would a partner's interview.

### Thank You Notes

The thank you note is an extremely effective strategy that will hold you in good stead when you interview with *everyone* in the interviewing process.

They can be short and friendly:

Dear Ms. Jones:

Thanks for the time you spent with me yesterday. I enjoyed talking to you about your practice and feel I could be an effective part of your team.

Dear Mr. Smith:

Thanks for the interview on Wednesday. I hope we can work together in the near future. I look forward to your high-energy office atmosphere.

Mail a little Hallmark card to everyone with whom you interview. Everyone. The *thank you note* falls under the category of **"Highly recommended, but highly neglected."** It can act as an "extra salute" to someone, or a "patch" on an area you might have neglected, or a "restatement" of enthusiasm and interest you might have underplayed. In any case, in this context it helps you remember the political terrain upon which you are treading. It is important to know this terrain, since you might be walking it for years after you are hired.

### Each Firm Is Different

Just knowing that firm politics may have an impact on your hiring is not enough. You should do as much as you can at whatever stage you find yourself to discover as much as you can about the firm you are pursuing. If the firm is small and has been small for years, it might have a legal administrator/manager who is a spouse of one of the partners. It might have a group of partners who have been together for years and only hire associates to get them started, offering little chance of partnership. This kind of firm could be good for paralegal utilization and could have a very influential manager. Other configurations of firms might have different meanings, but hopefully all of your information goes to one goal: Filling in an incomplete picture so you can make intelligent moves toward your ultimate hiring.

Small firms have definite personalities. Life-style, politics, and socio-economics could fall into very clear patterns. A senior partner/owner in a small firm has a much more powerful impact on the personality and atmosphere of a place than one in a large firm. The *impact* of personality and style is very strong in a small setting. Questions you can ask that will help you learn quickly would be:

1) Is this a new firm or an older firm?
2) Is the firm's partnership made up of younger, middle-aged, or older individuals?
3) Do life-style and politics seem to be very important to this firm?
4) What is the make-up of the firm and staff (culture, gender, age, etc.)?
5) What do their practice area and client picture tell me about the firm and how to become a part of it?
6) Where is this firm located? What does that tell me? Is this a suburban, urban, or rural firm? How will those factors affect the political terrain, the firm personality, and the attitude toward paralegals?
7) Once I have a picture of this firm and get an idea of how they utilize their paralegals, what will I emphasize in my letters, networking, telephoning, and interviewing?

### The Paralegal Role in Small and Midsize Firms

While sole practitioners utilize paralegals in the way they feel they "have to in order to keep their practice going," the small and midsized firms can differ radically from each other, based upon attorney attitudes, professional habits, practice area, and the attorney/paralegal ratio. Among the attorneys you may encounter:

1) those who are just now acknowledging that paralegals are out there and doing something special
2) those who believe paralegals are "glorified secretaries"
3) those who use paralegals for all office-support functions

4) those who hold paralegals in high esteem and are very mindful of the workload and kind of work paralegals do

5) those who believe in the profitability of paralegals and keep their attorney/paralegal ratio at such a level as to put much of the weight of their practice on the paralegal function

6) those who attempt to keep their valued paralegals as "virtual partners" by rewarding them with a full array of benefits, bonuses, and high wages

As the paralegal profession grows and makes gains in nontraditional and traditional areas alike, there is a gradual lessening of old, entrenched attitudes and an increasing growth of enlightened attitudes. Still, be forewarned that in your experience you can find every attitude toward paralegals as you go through your career.

The small and midsize firm does not generally have the fixed corporate policies of large firms. It is here that you, as a future paralegal, will discover the widest range of existing attitudes and philosophies about paralegal roles. One firm will value its paralegals because they are heavily used in client contact, others use their paralegals in case management. Still others use their paralegals in a much broader way, treating them not unlike paralegals in a sole proprietorship. In any case, the challenge is to understand as early as possible how paralegals are utilized so that you can adjust your presentation to fit the need.

## Summary: Issues to consider when facing a small firm

Understand the *organizational structure*, particularly:

♦ the contact person whom you must discover and communicate with
♦ the possibility of networking with an associate, partner, or other paralegal in the office
♦ the usefulness of thank you notes, cover letters, and follow-up phone calls

Learn the *individual terrain* of the particular firm you are pursuing and its specific personality by:

♦ asking meaningful and specific questions about the firm
♦ understanding how paralegal utilization varies in these firms depending on their personality and style and degree of sophistication, and endeavor to fit that particular mold

## *The large law firm*

The large firm varies by number and city and region. Suffice it to say that "large firm" probably has a specific bottom number of attorneys, like 50 in a medium-sized city, or 100 to 200 or more in a larger city. A large firm, from a placement and job hunting point of view, is one that is the *largest* in a given area. In stricter terms, it is a firm with a broad base of clients; it has practice areas with teams of partners, attorneys, and paralegals who often work in what are called "pods" (to use a newer term); it is highly structured and has broad corporate and personnel policies. Often, they employ a Human Resources professional and have "Hiring Committees" with designated attorneys as "chairman." These responsibilities change over the years as people rotate in and out of different functions. Large firms are very much like modern corporations and differ from the sole practitioner and smaller firm in kind. Yes, they practice law, but in almost every other way they differ as places of employment.

### *The Paralegal in a Large Firm*

In a large firm most paralegals will have their own offices. This is a benefit indeed. Paralegal work in a large firm is highly delineated and compartmentalized. Some do "case management," which for many paralegals is very satisfying and rewarding. Others, after they reach large firms, long for the days when they had the greater independence and variety of the smaller setting. A "bankruptcy paralegal" in a large firm might manage large Chapter 11's, be an expert on Dbase or Lotus, and manage cases with very large numbers of documents. The debtor bankruptcy practice of a sole proprietor bears little resemblance to this. A real estate paralegal in a large firm might be handling scores of foreclosures or immense commercial transactions—work that can be fraught with pressure and tension, providing the stimulation that many enjoy in the world of paralegal practice.

The stakes are higher in a large firm, or at least they seem so. The paralegal has a case load to manage, much like their own practice. Perhaps he or she will be interfacing with two or three different specialty areas. Some in large firms work only with a single team or practice area. The challenge in a large firm is to be "busy, but not too busy." There is only so much control you have over your own life, but the key lies largely in diplomacy and the ability to be efficient. At times you can say "No" to work if you are overloaded. Trying to gauge work level is the continual mission in a large law firm:

1) How busy am I right now?
2) How busy will I stay at this current level?
3) If a case settles, will I have enough work?
4) Maybe I should say "yes" to all the new work.
5) Maybe I should always say "yes" to all the work offered me.
6) How can I get into other practice areas in the firm?
7) Can I meet my monthly billing requirements every month this year? Are layoffs a possibility?

Many large firms only hire paralegals with experience. An entry paralegal is often not considered because the large firm wants to see that you have been trained as a paralegal and know enough about the legal world and its standards to survive and succeed in a professional setting such as theirs. Occasionally, however, large firms will specifically advertise for recently graduated paralegals to work on large cases requiring litigation support assistance. These positions are often titled "Case Assistant," "File Clerk," "Document Clerk," etc. In these circumstances, apply if you are prepared to take a lower salary but want the chance to get established with a "name" firm.

How does an entry paralegal get into a large firm? Network through a friend, or the relative of a firm member, or the friend of a friend, or relative of an associate. Sometimes large firms go through agencies so that they do not have to interview until the end of the process. One entry paralegal got on with a large firm through a skiing club.

The myth that large firms have the best pay often draws paralegals to large firms. Only then do they discover that large firms did not get large by throwing money around. They discover that pay policies are more structured and that raises are predictable and fixed (within a range). They discover that they will be paid well the longer they remain with the large firm, but that a large firm can be tough to negotiate with when discussing initial employment. The large law firm offers its reputation, good benefits, relative security, and a comfortable environment in which to labor.

The large firm can be impersonal, and at times the paralegal can feel anonymous. The friendliness and team spirit of a smaller entity is just not there. The large firm should be viewed as a goal that many reach, but it should also be seen as a goal that might dash expectations. Large firms are simply like everything else we have been covering—a place in which there is benefit and risk, good and bad. The more you know and discover before making a decision, and the sharper your eyes are as you proceed through your career, the better off you will be.

# Politics—The Unseen Hand

*If I could not go to heaven but with a (political) party, I would not go there at all.*

Thomas Jefferson

I have referred to the importance of *practice area* in determining the kind of work you get and the levels of responsibility to which you might rise. For instance, certain practice areas lend themselves to large documentation, while others present you with more client contact. We have not yet discussed how *personal politics or viewpoints* might affect your hiring. While no one should ask your political allegiance or party affiliation, there is something to note as you conduct your job search campaign. Out there in the rough and tumble of the law, political point of view plays a role.

While a paralegal's personal beliefs are officially unimportant, paralegals can disqualify themselves in interviews by making remarks that fall on the "wrong side of the fence." A naive applicant should avoid making comments about practice areas and plaintiff vs. defendant issues until that applicant discovers:

1) Does the firm handle only Plaintiffs?
2) Is this a Defense firm?
3) Does this firm handle both sides?

The truth is that most paralegals keep their personal politics and philosophies to themselves so that they can remain employable and economically viable. Some get uncomfortable doing one kind of work (Plaintiff or Defense), and then quietly work their way toward a firm where things are more congenial to their mindset.

## Plaintiff and defense

There are some paralegals who by life-style, fashion, and general demeanor consciously align themselves politically, declaring to everyone where their sentiments lie. That is fine as long as applicants are aware of their conduct and only want to work in a certain area of the law. The challenge for most of us who want to have broad acceptability is to look as neutral and sound as unaligned as possible when writing and interviewing.

Those who come into the legal world with the word "environmental" on their lips are generally speaking philosophically of one side, and do not realize that many "environmental" jobs are on the other.

There are two sides to the practice area called "criminal": defense and prosecution. Some people will work both sides, and some will only work for the district attorney. Others' sympathies come down on the defense side. Defense firms are so named because they generally represent large corporations, insurance companies, and "deep pocket" clients (a common term for wealth). A lawsuit generally comes about because deep pockets have been discovered. A Plaintiff's firm is in business to take up the cause of a smaller company or an individual or group of individuals who feel they have been wronged in some way. This is the simplest of pictures to describe what happens in this adversarial system we have constructed. You as the singular applicant do not have to learn an elaborate coded language or understand these dynamics at their most sophisticated level. You only need to appear as "unpolitical" as possible and be able to handle some questions. You may get questions like:

1) How do you feel about working for a criminal defense firm?
2) If you've had nursing experience, how do you feel about defending doctors?
3) Our firm is full of activists and we take on churches and large corporations. How do you feel about that?

## *"Wolf in sheep's clothing"*

The hiring of a new paralegal brings a professional into a team in the middle of adversarial contests. The team concept is implicit in your job description. The firm wants to feel you will be a part of the team. In the intense competition for available openings, the applicant who appears the most sympathetic, or even the most innocuous and neutral, is probably going to be considered and hired over a person who creates some doubt about his or her polarities. You do not need to play a cheerleader game either. Do not attempt to be more ardent than the already ardent. The best image is that of professionalism, neutrality, and objectivity. Sympathy for "our side" is a natural process that will arise in any effort after you are hired and going to trial. Do not drum up sentiments you do not have. The main goal is not to look like a "wolf in sheep's clothing."

Mind you, if you disguise your true sentiments about something in order to get hired, and then you spout off continually about it, you will probably end up unemployed anyway. Under the umbrella of professionalism is a smaller word—*discretion.* If you have this quality as you employ your opening moves and use job strategies, you will surely benefit yourself.

## Finding the Job You Want: Advertised and Unadvertised Leads

Now that we have concluded discussions about the (1) sole practitioner, (2) small and medium firms, and (3) large firms, the proper attitude of the professional job hunter, and the importance of understanding the political terrain in the legal profession, let us turn to the kinds of opportunities you will encounter.

Strategies and first moves after graduation lead one naturally to a discussion about how to approach the advertised market and the unadvertised or "hidden" job market. Various studies have put the "hidden market" at 70-80 percent of the existing market for any given profession. A good opening strategy is to decide that you are not going to ignore the larger market. However, many people in entry-level circumstances have one strategy: Wake up by 10:00 A.M. on Sunday morning, check under "L" and "P," write some cover letters, and wait until next week.

There is a way of dealing with both the advertised market and the unadvertised market *simultaneously*. Advertised leads are "easy to find" because they are announced through some means, but they are "hard to get" because all those looking are put on notice to apply. Thus the competition is more furious and intense with an advertised lead. An unadvertised opening is one you discover through the various methods we will be describing. It is "hard to find" but "easier to get" because the competition is either minimal or nonexistent. With a networked opening, the work is all up front and, by the time you are interviewing, you are virtually in. You have been prequalified and there is a strong interest in you. And that's before your first interview!

### *Every moth was once a caterpillar*

Most advertised leads you see in a paper were once openings in the unadvertised category. The evolution of a lead is such that many openings never even make it to the networking stage. Many are announced at a lunch in a paralegal association meeting, a friend tells another she is moving to another city, and they tell a third who has been wanting to leave her firm for several weeks. She quietly interviews and then gives notice after receiving an offer. It all happens before it's even announced. Or an entry paralegal who joins an association hears about a big case for which assistance will be needed. With the help of the paralegal friend, the new paralegal writes a letter to the attorney involved and an opening is filled, again, before it is "announced."

Once an opening is in the networking category, it could stay that way for a time if the workload does not demand an immediate replacement. This is usually the main determinant of a "networking situation" going to the "advertised" category. It is simply the extremity of need that makes people go to the advertised market. Then, often, schools and associations are the first ones to hear before the newspaper does. When the newspaper gets the lead, the unqualified, the qualified, and the remotely qualified apply, inundating the firm with cover letters and resumes.

### The opening that isn't an opening until the person and the timing are right

Some openings do not proceed to the level of extreme need because other support personnel are taking up the work. Legal work is such that by pushing it around artfully a smaller staff can handle it. Loyal and professional paralegals take up the slack by working harder and the firm goes on without worrying about hiring. The message is, "We are not going to replace Sally right away, we think the staff will be able to handle the upcoming workload."

And so the opening is there. But it's not there. Management puts off the decision until a later date and time goes on. Then in a few months, maybe the work increases and the staff starts to communicate their feelings about the need for a "replacement of Sally"; and then, management may start to "unofficially look." If your *direct mail letter*, by sheer coincidence, arrives on a certain contact person's desk at this time, they pick up the phone and ask you to come in. And a star is born.

### Networking—the way around the labyrinth and into the inner sanctum

> The Front Door may be just as close
> To the Inner Sanctum
> As The Back Door,
> But there is a
> Labyrinth
> At The Front Door

Everyone knows of the old saying, "It's not what you know, but who you know, that counts." That does not tell the whole story. It is what you know *and* who you know that matters in the law. Networking can be a valuable skill. The key elements of successful networking can be summarized as follows:

**1) Tell everyone.**   Tell every friend and relative that you are in the business of networking attorneys and paralegals and law firms.

**2) Utilize a direct mail program.**   Use a regular weekly system to develop leads, contacts, and informational interviews.

**3) Associate.**   Join every professional association for which you are eligible and go to their meetings.

**4) Socialize.**   Put yourself in the right social settings to meet people.

**5) Dress for success.**   Dress for the job that you are aspiring to. Underdressing for any event is a felony; overdressing is a minor misdemeanor.

**6) Develop interviews whenever possible.**   Every circumstance in which you find yourself—baseball games, church socials, family picnics—all provide a chance to get a name, to write a letter, to perhaps get five minutes of someone's time to talk about opportunities in a given practice area.

**7) The "Backward Cousin" Rule.**   Everyone has an enemy or two. Maybe it is someone you pushed too far, or someone who pushed you too far. A "backward cousin," if you will, one who you swore you would avoid at all costs. Invigorate that relationship. Swallow your pride and see if that old friend or backward cousin might have a connection. It couldn't hurt. Anyone and everyone can know a lawyer.

**8) Use a job search journal.**   Log everything you do. Keep a record of the entire effort that you have undertaken. Have one three-inch binder that contains every name, address, advertisement, beer-stained napkin, or coffee-stained envelope. This journal will be your bible and your organizer. Knowing this helps allay inner fears and nerves.

While we will have much more to say about networking and direct mail later on, this early emphasis is to alert you to integrate this into a grand strategy for yourself, so that you can dive into the frenzied and stimulating life of a full-time job hunter. It must be your strategy to embrace this concept of professional networking from the very beginning. If you do not believe in it, you probably will not undertake it. It is a job that requires hustle!

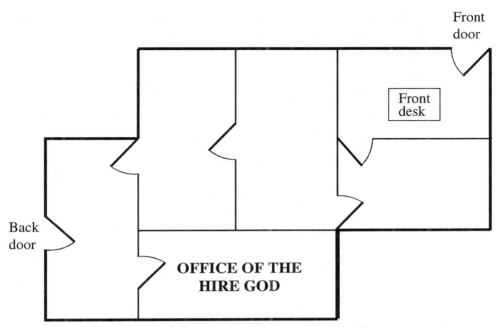

Front
door

Front
desk

Back
door

**OFFICE OF THE
HIRE GOD**

**Fig. 3-2** Advantages of networking or "going through the back door."

## H.U.S.T.L.E.

The final strategy has to do with the quality of your effort. Very little of this comes naturally . . . unless you are a natural hustler. The first spirit of America is fierce independence. The fiercely independent declared that without the shackles of the old world binding a person to a state or class, an individual by dint of competition, energy, drive, and persistence could and would succeed at any fully engaged endeavor. That ideal still exists. In fact it is never more true than in the Synergistic Job Search. If there is any natural order that emerges in this realm, it is the one that says: Those who must survive and succeed will!

Simply outlining the basics of networking and delving into the myriad details of the job hunt will not aid you without your unqualified effort. If you hustle, you will notice how you are building a circuit of contacts that take on a life; you are planting a crop that will eventually yield a harvest. In the end, this book is not only about getting your first job, but subscribing to the idea that your self-development and your professional development go together. We are all interconnected and interdependent—not unlike the law. **The concept of *hustling* involves the self-**  **awareness that your future is always being planned for you, uncon-**

sciously or consciously, by your daily effort and by the interconnectedness of your daily professional life.

---

**HIT THE STREETS**

**USE EVERY MOVE**

**STAY COOL**

**TELL EVERYBODY**

**LET THINGS BE**

**EXPECT GOOD NEWS**

---

### *H* Is for "Hit the Streets"

The truly competitive person is out there shaking hands, having lunch, and meeting people. You will be sitting down and discussing your profession with people from whom you can learn. These people will constitute your network. Those who try to hunt for a job solely by responding to ads are not hitting the streets. Go out on every interview you get; the experience of interviewing is invaluable, and it is difficult to fabricate. Any interview, even a bad one, can be useful experience.

### *U* Is for "Use Every Move"

I am not speaking of moves that are outside ethical and professional standards. We should use all the legitimate methods that work in the job hunting process. Some people use only half the methods available to them because they are lazy or reluctant or disbelieving. Those who hustle are headed for their goal; for example, the idea of writing a thank you note is not that hard to do because their focus is on the big picture.

### *S* Is for "Stay Cool"

Anyone who is an entrepreneur or salesman can tell you that you cannot permit yourself to look hungry. Perceived hunger has a way of driving people away. As you proceed with your job hunt, look the part, feel the part, dress the part, act the part of a professional paralegal.

(Remember, you are in the self-promotion business at this point.) You always want to communicate the message and exude the confidence of someone who will "be a catch." If you do not stay cool, your energy and hustle will work against you.

### *T Is for "Tell Everybody"*

The hunt for your first job is actually even more than a job. It is an occupation, even a *preoccupation*. Though you should stay cool, your agenda should be jammed with one message: "I must tell everyone who cares about me what I am doing." This time might be a time to lose some false pride, because one thing this quest will show you is that you do not know where your fortune will come from. When something starts to work, you may be amazed at its originating point.

### *L Is for "Let Things Be"*

Waiting is a hard game, and it may go against your natural drive to *"do something,"* but remember the analogy of the crop coming in. You cannot coax a seed to sprout, nor yell at a plant to make it flower. The whole process requires time and waiting and patience; you'll make good moves, then wait. Like an echo, your job search efforts have a response time. Some may be one week, others two days, still others may take three months. How do you stay cool? By knowing there is a process going on. This is one of the reasons you should undertake a great deal and work hard on several projects. The crop sometimes comes in all at once. Sometimes nothing happens for weeks, and then by some eerie synchronicity, everyone seems to be interested at once. But remember, do not become a pure nuisance by calling back too much on a lead. After you have done what you can, let things be.

### *E Is for "Expect Good News"*

The job hunt is emotionally arduous because you must be at your best when you often feel your worst. Undertake this process with the most optimistic outlook you can muster. Why? Because it affects your daily performance, your interviewing, your writing, your personal networking, your sense of worth, and your professionalism. All these things are buoyed by your optimism. The true hustler can see the results of worthwhile activity, just as the farmer sees the crop coming in when he is plowing, digging and dunging, and watching it rain. Some of the worst interviews occur because the interviewee is exhausted emotionally and fighting self-doubt and discouragement. One of your chief strategies and opening moves is to begin with (and stay in) a state of hopeful and optimistic expectation.

Once you are prepared to undertake this task with the proper opening strategies and first moves, then you can employ your resume, interviewing skills, and written presentations with persuasion and effectiveness.

> All the effort, education, handshaking
> Telephoning, letter-writing, hand-wringing
> And stamp-licking
> Come together in one moment:
> Your interview.

# CHAPTER 4

---

## *The Effective Legal Interview*
### *Getting Hired*

A quiet breeze blew across the outdoor patio at our favorite down-town cafe. My colleague continued to stir the cream into her coffee as she talked. "You know, most paralegal applicants have a good array of skills and wonderful personalities. The interview is just the place where some are more effective than others at getting their skills and their personalities across." She had spent several years counseling paralegal graduates; her musings were part of an extended conversation about the legal interview. She leaned forward, as if she were telling a secret. "It's really true. Sometimes the jobs just go to the best interviewees, and yet it just takes a little work to become a good interviewee!" We finished the lunch concluding that new paralegals face *two challenges.* Not only do paralegals face the most obvious challenge of interviewing for employment, but, at the same time, they must gain access to a new and special profession through that interview.

Getting ready for, going to, and participating in an interview is challenging, nerve-wracking, and for some, dreadful. Yet the formal interview is the way people get work. In fact, the majority of the hiring process takes place in the interview. There are enough other factors in the interview process to make it the palm-moistening, mouth-drying event that it is, but that factor alone turns knees into Jello and sets hearts aflutter. It helps sometimes to ponder the elements involved. As one student, with a sense of humor, put it,

> First, it's like public speaking, so it makes you sweat even if you're enjoying it. Then, it's personal stuff about yourself, and that makes most of us very uncomfortable. Then, we realize that "they're interviewing lots

of others, too" and this builds resentment, and after all this, we say "yeah, but what if they want me?!"

When you think about it this way, you wonder how people do as well as they do in the interview process.

Throw in, then, the additional challenge of entering a new world—the legal profession—and we have this double challenge. Thousands of paralegals have faced these challenges successfully over the last two decades, but it still remains a special assignment.

## The Effective Legal Interview

Let's construct a working definition of an *effective legal interview* so that we can show how the aspiring paralegal can face this dual challenge. Following this definition will give you a successful formula for planning a winning presentation in the interview:

> An effective legal interview is a warm, enthusiastic, and poised presentation of your qualifications, background, and skills as they relate to the legal profession. Your professional persona should reflect standards and values consistent with the legal profession. Your well-constructed presentation is directed and focused upon a specific *job* and *firm*, as you work to build a mutual intensity of interest that culminates in a feeling and a sense that you could be a part of the team.

Now, let's examine several elements of this definition.

- ◆ **"Warm and Enthusiastic"**    In an interview, you must believe that all of your past experiences and situations have come together to build a fine professional candidate who is worthy of consideration. The presentation you make must be made with self-esteem, strength, a positive attitude, and a glowing sense that you are a worthy candidate. Even though the field of law might seem a bit intimidating at first, be assured that meekness, weakness, or an unsure approach are generally ineffective in an interview.

- ◆ **"Poised Presentation"**    All new paralegals should be sure of the content of their background, education, skills, and other pertinent parts of their presentations. The more familiar you are with this "tale," the more poised you will be in making it. There is nothing wrong with a little rehearsal.

- **"Of Your Qualifications, Background, and Skills"**    What many people's presentations lack is knowing how to transfer their skills to the present job opportunity. A legal interview should go to legal concerns. The simple chronological recounting of the events of your life, without "filtering" it for legal and paralegal issues, can sound like you are only in need of a job and have nothing of special value to bring to the position.

- **"And Your Professional Persona"**    Along with the proper clothing, your demeanor should reflect a person who is up to the challenge of the world of the law. This may require an extra dose of confidence, but for some it also might require extra restraint and seriousness. You should reflect the middle road of confidence and stability. There are as many people who come on too strong as come on too weak.

- **"Focused on Specific Job and Firm"**    Many job seekers do not *listen* while the interview is going on. A lot of essential information is given *during* the interview which helps the creative and responsible job seeker design the presentation for both the job being described and the firm in which they are interviewing. Remember, you are trying to get invited to be a part of a "professional family." You must gear your presentations to both the job and the environment and people in which that job will take place.

- **"Mutual Intensity of Interest"**    The effective legal interview is an *active* process. If you passively participate in the interview, such as by simply answering questions you are asked, you are missing an opportunity to build enthusiasm on your part and theirs. Often the person who is hired is the one who was able to express the most interest in the job and get the hiring firm excited about their interest. As one recent hire put it, "I knew I had the job when they got as excited as I was. It was almost as if my enthusiasm was reflected back to me, and then it turned into an offer."

- **"A Part of the Team"**    Because the special world of the law has some characteristics that make it unique, the "team" is a strong concept. The need for confidentiality creates in firm members the realization that they can only talk with their coworkers about their work. The high stakes, win-lose atmosphere also offers camaraderie among firm members. This is true of all work settings, but it is especially true of the high drama, confidentiality, competitiveness, and tension of the law. When you interview for a job as a paralegal, you are not trying to get a spot on a production line, performing one highly skilled task. You are trying to join a small group of people who will be working very closely together under varying circumstances in an array of work situations. The people you interview with will be looking at your skills and qualifications, but they will also be looking at your potential as a team player. This is an aspect of the legal interview that unsuccessful interviewees often forget, and successful job seekers have in the forefront of their minds.

## Interviewing in the World of the Law Firm

Five particular characteristics bear on hiring practices. Once you have worked in the legal environment for a time, these characteristics will just seem like normal descriptions of the professional terrain; when you are new, they can befuddle and confuse you, cause apprehension, and perhaps keep you from getting hired for a job that you really wanted.  **Often, the challenge of getting hired for your first paralegal job will be to fit into the special individuality of a small firm.** Since many entry paralegal jobs are with sole practitioners and small firms, you must be ready to quickly analyze a host of factors from location, practice area, personality types, and age of the firm. Most important, do not interview with preconceptions about the firm's individuality and personal style.

### Individuality vs. homogeneity

Law firms are entrepreneurial professional practices that grow into various sizes and cultures. They all have a unique style and personality. They cultivate a special individuality and do not attempt the same look or identity. The personalities of the founding dominant partners will determine much of that special flavor. Some firms will be quiet and austere, others manic and active; some will be relaxed and friendly, others will be uptown, downtown, or suburban in attitude or style. The point here is that you cannot count on any one consistent kind of look for law firms.

### Conservative and traditional

You may find some urban firms where you will see long hair, open collars, and a relaxed style, but those are exceptions. Expect to see a conservative and traditional world. Even with their unique personalities, styles, and cultures, law firms are still conservative and traditional. In the interview phase, in which you are still a stranger, you must hold to the image that the world you are entering was built upon generations of laws, cases, social values, political systems, and certain unwavering standards.

The effective legal interview is one that sounds and feels like a dialogue with an associate in the firm. You must educate yourself on terminology, buzz words, nomenclature, and vocabulary that is of that world. Study Chapter 2 for descriptions of typical kinds of job situations. Review your class notes and texts so that you can prepare yourself for specific kinds of practice area discussions. Immerse yourself in internship or externship experiences so that you can learn the language of those involved in the daily business of a dynamic, busy law office. Just remember that you, as the employable paralegal, should interview as a good solid citizen, an individual of strong values and standards, and a reliable person.

### Serious and earnest

You will discover as you interview and, eventually, work in the field of law that everyone is in earnest about their practices. The law is a place where disputes are settled and business is done. Money is almost always passing hands and lives are always being affected. In this environment, people get serious. Everyone "plays for keeps." It does not matter if the lawsuit is about a dog bite or custody of a favorite cat—it's a lawsuit! One of the keys to effective interviewing is to reflect your seriousness without being grave. Be warm, without being flip. Get people to talk about their practices—most everyone loves to talk about their practice, and they definitely love to talk to people who are interested in that practice. One paralegal graduate recently said, "I was told I was hired because I was the most interested in the practice area."

### Deadline-oriented

One attorney seeking to make a point in an interview once said, "If 3:00 on Tuesday afternoon is our deadline, then that is the most important date that week. Work in this place happens when it happens. You must be ready for it." The world you are now entering can get dramatic and intense at any time, on any day, depending upon the docket. The work flow is not predictable. As a successful interviewee, you must portray yourself as practical, hardworking, and eager to get the job done.

### Exclusivity

Lawyers are in a special group. They went to law school and passed into a community of professionals. The firms that arise from this community of professionals have an exclusivity about them. Paralegals have educational and experiential requirements. Legal secretaries also have extensive training and experiential requirements. New paralegals must present themselves as professionals, but understand that they are not yet a part of the club. Law firms are teams of tightly knit professionals who have all become familiar with one another and have become accustomed to each others' behaviors and patterns. When a new person joins this "family," the real test (after qualifying them) is whether they think they will be able to get along with the new person. An interviewee who communicates an attractive warmth, ease, and diplomacy will probably have an edge.

You should be seeing a clear picture of law firms developing, as each of these qualities works off the other. **Law firms tend to be individuated, deadline-oriented, serious places that are conservative and intense, populated with teams of highly trained professionals who must work closely with one another and face changing and sometimes dramatic work flow changes. This description by no means pretends to depict the totality of law firm life, but these factors are paramount in the interview process.** The well-trained and prepared paralegal applicant considers these elements when constructing his or her presentations.

## Types of Legal Interviews

With the definition of an effective legal interview discussed earlier in mind, and an appreciation for some of the main characteristics of the legal environment into which you are seeking entrance, let's now consider some basic kinds of interviews that you may encounter.

### The nonadversarial chat

This is a very common kind of interview. Friendly and apparently unorganized, it is decidedly nonadversarial and relaxed. The interviewer may seem to jump around from subject to subject. They talk about one aspect of the job, then they will talk about a strong personality in the office, then they will ask a question of the interviewee. The interview will tend to meander like this. Keep in mind that the interviewer does have priorities, even if they are difficult to discern. You need to read between the lines and avoid becoming lax or complacent about the interview. Assume that the questions the interviewer comes back to are the ones he or she cares about. Highlight different aspects of your background or a key skill for what seems to be revealing itself in the interview. It is easy to feel you have done well, or feel unsure about your performance in the

Table 4.1.  Types of Legal Interviews

|  | THE NONADVER-SARIAL CHAT | THE CROSS-EXAMINATION | THE COURT OF INQUIRY |
|---|---|---|---|
| Characteristics | friendly<br>apparently nondi-rected | organized<br>cool<br>tense | groups of inter-viewers<br>multiple kinds of questions |
| Trap/Pitfall | too relaxed<br>unaware of real agenda | timidity<br>unsureness | to become overwhelmed<br>to reveal too much of self<br>to answer incom-pletely |
| Solution | keep alert<br>stay with your bio<br>be upbeat | do not overreact to negative tension<br>present yourself positively<br>be positive and assertive | enjoy the ride<br>keep a smile on your face<br>don't rush answers |

nonadversarial chat. With this kind of interview, seldom do you feel you have done poorly.

## The cross-examination

This interview is organized and methodical. Often the interviewer is using written notes and materials. The interviewer does not seem to care whether you feel comfortable or not. He or she might make an attempt to be friendly, but you have the feeling it is because their notes probably told them to. Don't be rattled; try to give complete responses. Do not over-answer or grope for answers trying to respond too completely. These interviews test your mettle and your enthusiasm. You can easily feel you have done poorly in these interviews. You may do very well, in fact, but feel terrible. Do not be disturbed. One of the purposes for this kind of interview is to determine if you can handle the pressure. Remember, these interviewers are deliberately not showing many feelings.

## The court of inquiry

Interviews with two, three, or more people are inherently difficult because you are dealing with different styles and personalities, which may range from gushy to friendly to distant to malicious—all in the same room. The key here is to remember your strengths, and enjoy. If one person rattles you, at least you can take solace in the fact that someone else's question will be coming up soon. You can have fun with these interviews. One person recently said that she feels she can "work the room" with this type of interview. Humor often works best in these interviews. A group feeling develops that can work for you if it goes well. Unfortunately, those who are timid can appear absolutely mute unless they have practiced and developed an interview mind set that keeps their attitude upbeat.

## Interviewing Style

Contrary to what you may have heard, the legal interview is not a lion's den, but an arena with special qualities. The special qualities affect both *style* and *kind.* We've just looked at the kinds of interviews; now, let's consider different styles. Be conscious of the style, but don't get taken in by style. "Style," as opposed to "kind," has more to do with the individual's approach to you and not to the interviewing situation.

### The disarming, charming, nonalarming style

*Most* legal interviews are very pleasant and positive experiences. Most nonadversarial chats are conducted by those who are "disarming, charming, and nonalarming." Attorneys are excellent at getting the relaxation response from job candidates. This is generally good, because the interviewees tend to relax and perform in a confident manner. The caveat here is that interviewees relax too much, reveal too much, open up too much, and generally talk too much. Answers become overly long and meandering. It is almost as if the relief felt in the interview causes an overly familiar style that, in the end, offends. Keep your composure at all times in the interview process, no matter how relieved and elated you may feel.

### The distant, remote, cool style

If someone is remote and cold, don't respond in kind. Try to measure your responses and temper yourself, but do not be dragged down by the gravity of their dignified bearing. Stick to your bio, be yourself, sell your skills, and stay upbeat and enthusiastic. Those who are too nervous will probably be muted by this style and thus descend into quietude. The cocky and nervous will chatter and could disqualify themselves. It is the composed, upbeat, positive, and buoyant interview that will make an impression.

## The professorial style

If a lawyer or administrator gives you a "mini bar exam" and tests your memory and intellect, do your best, but get in your story, stay enthusiastic, and don't lose your cool. If your memory serves you well and you know all the answers, very good. If your memory does not serve you well, talk about how the paralegal knows where to find the answer and has the willingness to pursue a question until she gets an answer. The worst response is to gnarl up inside and get red-faced because you are not passing their test. Remember, you do not know how other candidates have fared: It may be a test of your poise as much as of your knowledge.

## The distracted, irritated, gruff style

Many attorneys interview "on the run," in the middle of their busy day. If someone is distracted, antagonistic, and gruff, it is probably a matter of temperament and a busy schedule. Do not take it personally. Keep your poise, stay professional, generate enthusiasm, call it an adventure, and do your best. Those who interview this way do so because their day is one up-and-down roller coaster ride, and they are taking just a few minutes out to talk to you. If you get your story in and declare your virtues positively, the interviewer may be very impressed. You must get this interviewer's attention with a professional presentation. A muted and intimidated presentation will not win the day.

# The Four Parts of a Legal Interview

Those who leave the interview to fate seem to think that the interview is just one long series of questions and answers. The winning presentations are most often given by paralegals who understand the basic structure of an effective legal interview.

## The warm-up

The warm-up is actually the most important part of the interview. It comes first and it is the mood setter. A good beginning will have a positive effect on the whole interview. The first five minutes of an interview are the most important. This is very much like a blind date, for it is the first few minutes when people are sizing up, getting feelings, and getting comfortable with one another (more on this later in the chapter). If you know how to exude warmth, this would not be a bad time to glow.

Remember, interviewers get nervous too. If you can do your best to let them feel at ease, you will be getting the qualification mechanism working right away. It is only natural to like someone who has made you feel at ease. You gain if the interview goes well. This is when your enthusiasm headlights should be on "high beam." Gooey, gushy, and syrupy do not work, but there should be "warm" in the warm-up as an insurance policy for a successful interview.

### Their question, your answer

This is the part of the interview that many consider to be the entire interview. They pass the warm-up and go straight to business. The question-and-answer period should be as friendly and warm as possible. The more Gestapo-like this becomes, the less the "blind date" is working for you. Below we'll discuss typical kinds of questions you will get, but you must also consider the logical points of interest people will find in your resume, bio, and cover letter. Also, look at yourself honestly. Consider where your gaps or weaknesses are, and where potential areas of concern might lie. Do not assume that because someone is focusing on a gap or an area of weakness that they do not favor you. If a person is hoping to hire you, they may be particularly interested in potential weaknesses so that they can make a good case for you in a later meeting. Remember, the more you have dealt assertively with gaps and weaknesses in your bio, the less you will have to entertain questions about it in the Q&A.

The following is a list of often-asked interview questions that you may want to consider before each interview.

## FREQUENTLY ASKED LEGAL INTERVIEW QUESTIONS

1. Why do you (with your background) think you can be a paralegal?
2. Have you ever done this type of work (practice area) before?
3. Why did you choose the field of law?
4. Tell me about yourself.
5. Why do you want to be a _____ paralegal?
6. Why should we hire you?
7. What is your greatest strength?
8. What is your greatest weakness?
9. Five years from now, where would you like to be?
10. Do you really think you can handle _____ (least desirable feature of job)?

11. You seem to have changed jobs a lot.
12. How do you feel about a (male/female) boss?
13. What kind of person bothers you?
14. Why have you been out of work? (Gaps)
15. How are you with office politics?
16. How do you react when things get stressful?
17. If someone yells at you, what do you do?
18. Will you really work for this kind of money? (Asked of transitional people)
19. Do you want to be a lawyer?
20. How many years are you willing to give us?

### Your Questions, Their Answers

There is nothing wrong with coming in with a pad of paper and pen. If you have questions written down, this shows a degree of preparation that bespeaks professionalism and seriousness. Usually a good interviewer will answer most of your questions before you get a chance to ask them. One good global question that a paralegal can ask which seems natural and logical is, "How would you describe this firm's style as a home for a future employee?" or "What's it like to work here?" You should also ask specific questions you have about the nature of the practice and job. This will demonstrate your interest in the details of the position.

Questions that relate to the firm and the job description should be asked early in the interview process, demonstrating your interest in making a strong individual contribution. The area of job benefits may arise early as a standard part of the employer's presentation. Since the interviewee does not want to give the impression that they are only interested in the benefits, questions about benefits should be saved until the end of the interview process, near or at the tendering of an offer.

There are many questions you should be aware of and ready to ask — questions about compensation, overtime, billing rates (hard requirements and soft requirements), vacation, sick time, benefits, and times for review. Remember, never accept a job if there is any area of concern you have not explored. This is *your* responsibility. Ask the question in the interview or forever hold your peace. One person I counseled accepted a job based upon an assumption of paid overtime. But there was none — the firm paid no overtime. This disgruntled her. She said, "It just makes me mad that I failed to ask. It's not that I have to work that much OT."

### The Positive Conclusion: With a Bang, Not a Whimper

Studies show that most interviews wind down in a kind of anticlimactic fashion. They go out not with a bang, but with a whimper. Again this is the responsibility of the interviewee. If the interviewer orchestrates the interview to a resounding conclusion, that is good for you the interviewee, because you get a chance to repeat how much you enjoyed the talk, seeing the offices, and describing your background. But, if the interviewer does not know how to tell you that "It's over," you should grab the reins and positively conclude. Do it with a short recap of your qualifications and a truly sincere statement about wanting to meet them again, or even how you would like to have the job. This is the *close.* Salesmen know this word very well. You, at least, should end with a declarative statement of interest. This and the warm-up are very much the blind date part of the interview, and they tend to be neglected. In fact, the worst interviews do not have a warmup, questions from you or a successful conclusion, but are simply Their Q and Your A.

## Approaching the Legal Interview with a Sense of Responsibility

Because hiring is both subjective *and* objective, much of interviewing is out of our control. New paralegals must say: "I can affect certain things in this interviewing process, and there are many things I cannot affect. I am going to affect what I *can* affect." **The stage, the dialogue, the plot are all fairly predictable; the most important variable is your performance.** It is surely the main thing you can affect. As Shakespeare said through Cassius in "Julius Caesar":

> Men at some time are masters of their fates:
> The fault, dear Brutus, is not in our stars,
> But in ourselves, that we are underlings.

You can be the masters of your fate by preparing for the interview. And then, all the while, we can still live with the way the "cards are stacked." Consider that the interview is a card game. Imagine for a moment that you saunter into Dodge City and walk into the Long Branch Saloon. Kitty is smiling as you come in. Everyone at the card table is staring at you; their cards are against their chests. You sit. They know your name; you are introduced to them. As you set your weight into the chair, they say, "We'll tell you the game 'bit by bit.'" You smile and pick up your cards. The interview begins.

In spite of all variables that you cannot control, you still must embrace the interview process, as if you are fully and actively the master of your fate. It does not help to feel passive and fatalistic. The way to stay positive is to determine that you will prepare and that you will not succumb to the natural enemies that keep us from preparation.

## Warning: the primrose path to interviewing maladies

It is a strong temptation to let the interviewing process just happen. There are many reasons for this, but let us focus on four enemies to preparation. If you can avoid going down this primrose path, you can be well on your way to being an effective legal interviewee.

---

### THE PRIMROSE PATH TO INTERVIEWING MALADIES
#### Why it is "human" not to prepare well for interviews

**ENEMY #1**     The "natural" interview is a defeating myth.

**ENEMY #2**     "Fatalism" haunts the interview process.

**ENEMY #3**     The absence of a "feedback" system in the interview process gives you an illusion of success.

**ENEMY #4**     The job search is arduous; it's difficult to get "up" for the interview.

---

### Enemy #1—The "Natural Interview" Is a Defeating Myth

Yes, you must act "natural." And they will act "natural." And everyone will concentrate on being as friendly and warm as they can be to add to the atmosphere of "naturalness"; but in fact, the legal interview is *an unnatural contrivance!* We think, "I can't do anything but go in there and be my natural, witty, spontaneous self." This assumption is what creates a *lack of preparation.*

### Enemy #2—Fatalism Haunts the Interview Process

Working in tandem with this erroneous assumption that the interview is "natural," we have the basic fatalistic assumption of the potential paralegal: "If I am meant to get the job, it will go well; if it doesn't—oh, well, I wasn't meant to get the job." Expecting good fortune goes hand-in-hand with fatalism. The paralegal who is as prepared as possible can change the odds. This person creates more and better opportunities for self and career.

### Enemy #3—The Absence of a "Feedback" System Gives You an Illusion of Success

An unseen factor in the interview process is that you never know when you have done poorly. *Why* were you disqualified? Unless you *ask*, you will never know, and if you ask, most will not tell. So, when you hear people talk about interviewing, they are talking about their successes, which they can point to, and not their failures, which have not been disclosed to them.

### Enemy #4—The Job Search Process Is Arduous

Those who are fatalistic, anxious, and paralyzed about the job search process will probably have the same attitudes toward interviewing. Working on a polished presentation is your best prescription. (We will discuss this in more detail in the section on your bio below.) Just being optimistic and nervous is like whistling in the dark.

## Interview Performance: The Improvisational Theater

Having avoided the natural enemies to preparing well for an interview, we can move to taking full control and responsibility for our performance in the legal interview. Even the tenor and attitude of a decidedly dull interviewer, a distracted legal administrator, or a preoccupied attorney, can be changed. If the interviewer appears bored and unfocused, it's your job to make your interview go well. But remember, many legal interviewers take a "show me who you are" approach on purpose; they deliberately throw down the gauntlet to see how the interviewee responds.

For instance, imagine being faced with one or more of these questions. How would you answer?

"Well, Deborah, our paralegal position here is a kind of all-around support position, so why don't we start out with you: What can you tell me about yourself?"

"Samantha, I've had difficulties with paralegals being happy with me and my practice in the past. What do you think a good paralegal-attorney relationship would be? What kinds of duties are you looking for in a good paralegal job?"

"Well, David, why did you get into this profession, and what do you think you can do for me?"

"Sandra, tell me why you, in particular, would make a better paralegal than the other three, highly qualified candidates I have talked to this week. What makes you special?"

We will discuss several ways in which you can exercise positive control of the interview, but the basic element that you should have committed to a certain level of memory is the logical response to all four of the above questions. It is called "The Tale" or "The Bio" (which is short for biography). Whatever you choose to call it, it is *your story*.

The bio is the scripted and positive tale of your life, around which questions, answers, the job description, and the firm will circulate. It should be about two minutes in length, but it can be quickly reduced to 30 seconds if you concentrate on only the highlights. Regardless of its length, it is the basic answer to the question, "Why should I hire you?" Your bio should be loaded with *value* and *skills*. You are coloring a life and highlighting themes and hues, so that they all point to *legal*.

## At the improv

What I call "The Improvisational Theater of the Interview" is made up of the *text* and the *subtext*. The *text* is what is actually said during your interview. Like improvisational theater, this cannot be scripted in advance, but the actors (you and the interviewer) do follow some set guidelines that shape the text of the interview. The text usually is based on the following:

- ◆ the Job Description
- ◆ the Resume
- ◆ the Bio
- ◆ their Questions
- ◆ your Answers
- ◆ your Questions
- ◆ their Answers

The *subtext* is the visceral, emotional, subconscious, and subjective activity that occurs in your interview. Just as the scenery, costumes, and actors' mannerisms influence the audience's interpretation of the play, your appearance, your complexion, your body language, your eye contact, how much you squirmed, whether you had a cold, whether the interviewer found you visually appealing, will all affect the outcome of the interview. As much as you might want to cast your fate to the wind, there is still much you can do to be master of your fate. If a real improvisation goes well, the participants have a euphoria about this unique experience.

*That is often how a good interview goes*! If you read the actual text of a sour interview and a positive interview, you might not be able to tell which one was upbeat and which was downbeat. Often the judgment of an interview's success is passed at the tiniest moments—in the subtext, not the text. The success of an interview depends upon the emotional, subjective, and attitudinal elements: the genuineness of your smile; the authenticity of your eye contact; your posture and poise (or lack of it); the ease of your facial expressions; the winning way that you handle yourself; and the pure enthusiasm of your presentation; in short, in many subtle, physical, nonverbal ways.

The subtext is what goes on underneath the questions and answers, the carefully framed sentences and explanations. How can you influence the subtext? Like a good actor, you concentrate on the impression you are making through many things:

♦ **Your professional image**—clothing, manner, posture, gestures

♦ **Their perception of your image**—how you fit in with their team

♦ **Your interest**—expressed in direct eye contact, lively vocal variety

♦ **Moods and temperaments**—interview with upbeat and positive mood

♦ **Oral presentation**—strong, clear voice, little stumbling, no overlong pauses, not too loud or too soft, naturalness, no whispers or mumbling

♦ **Good body language**—erect posture, confident deliberate gestures

♦ **Bad body language**—nervous movements, stroking hair, fiddling mindlessly with fingers, articles of clothing, eyes darting back and forth, sudden jerky movements, slumped shoulders, inappropriate leg movements, furtive or distracting repetitive motions

## Summary: How to put it all together for the legal interview

Knowing who you are and what you want is essential. From that comes all the rest:

- Create the package. ("I am a young and ambitious, hardworking, well-qualified candidate with computer literacy and a real interest in investigations.")
- The bio should be framed to describe how the package came to be.
- How you adapt to the interviewing experience can create the perception that the firm has found "a match."
- Be comfortable and confident with yourself, but be ready to customize the interview on the spot.
- Your body language, eye contact, vocal variety, and dynamics must present an image of a confident professional.
- You will be hired on the basis of how your presentation matches your interviewing persona and how they fit the requirements of the firm.

## Interviewing Is an Art

A quiet, young woman with excellent grades was worried about the three or four dynamic personalities in her class. "How can I compete against them?" I told her, "You let them do their thing. You just be your best, most enthusiastic self!" She looked hopeful, but disbelieving. I continued, "Talking comes easier for some than others, but good interviewing is not just talking and sounding glib." An "easy talker" does not necessarily perform most effectively, especially in a paralegal interview.

Sometimes the glib interview is one of the reasons a person goes no farther in the interview process, yet the "easy talker" goes away in a self-congratulatory mood for having performed so well. Remember, there is little feedback in the world of interviewing. Who is going to tell you when you come on too strong? No one. They simply do not call you back.

When people are fortunate enough to get interviews, they must avoid falling into one of the two ditches that cause disqualification. Sometimes we overreact to the tension of the interview and either fall into a dreadful inferior silence or a chattering boastfulness.

| | |
|---|---|
| Inferiority ditch: | timid, shy, introverted, clammed up during the interview, insecure, overly nervous, taciturn |
| Superiority ditch: | overbearing, conceited, superior, showboat, cocky, offensive |

The inferior ditch and the superior ditch can actually occur in the same interview to the same interviewee. Why? They are both opposite reactions to the same two problems—lack of preparation and nervousness. No one goes to an interview telling themselves, "Now remember, be shy, timid, and insecure." Likewise, no one goes to an interview repeating to themselves, "Now don't forget to interrupt a great deal, talk too much, boast, act superior."

Both ditches are reactions to the tension and anticipation of the interview, but most of all they are a result of too little preparation. If you have a scripted and controlled presentation to make, and you know it well, your nervousness and tension will naturally lessen.

As we address the artistry of interviewing, it must be said that sheer warmth and enthusiasm count for a great deal. In the legal world, only the largest firms have human resource professionals, who have been professionally trained to interview and penetrate the warm fog of charm and extroversion that many interviewees perfect in the interview. People just tend to like a warm and enthusiastic person more than their cooler, shyer cousins. In short, be likeable and you have an edge. Warmth and charm that do not come off as arrogance will get you a long way in many situations.

There is an important job-based rationale here, too! If you interview with friendliness and enthusiasm as your banner, you will be perceived as one who understands that the role of paralegal is most successfully fulfilled by people who know that diplomacy and interpersonal sophistication are crucial to the paralegal role.

## The legal interview as a particular challenge

To get a wide perspective of the interview process, let us consider what makes paralegals valuable and appealing to lawyers.

- flexibility
- serious strong work ethic
- professionalism
- openness
- discretion
- enthusiasm
- diplomacy
- buoyancy
- ease
- looking the part
- common sense
- adaptability
- resourcefulness

Perhaps you can now see the utmost importance of being able to control your attitude for the interview. In the isolation of a vacuum we all meet these qualities in our own hearts and minds, but the question becomes, how much do we appear to have these qualities *when we interview?* You know you are a great potential employee, but do you sound like one when it counts?

Let us note the challenge you, the interviewee, face concerning attitude and demeanor as you enter the legal setting. Be your best professional paralegal self. Do not attempt to outlawyer the lawyer. Law firms come from a proud tradition of respectability, formality, and seriousness. It is a mistake to attempt to be more grave than your interviewer, but it is also a mistake not to be prepared to enter into this world with the proper decorum. Of course, you should not be overly casual and flippant, but most people forget that behind the mahogany furniture and well-tailored suits are regular people who drive on the same highways you do. Charm and likability will win you favor in a law firm, just as it will in a less "professional" setting.

## Preparing for the Effective Interview

### The bio

People often misunderstand the purpose of the bio. Skeptics say, "If it is scripted, it won't sound real." This is a problem of *presentation*, not memorization. It is true that people tend to sound robotic when they memorize something. I am not suggesting that you memorize your bio verbatim. However, it is a good idea to have a general outline in mind.

A young person's bio might sound something like this:

> I was a "Poli-Sci" major in college where I developed my initial interest in the law. I started reading about the paralegal profession and felt that my interests and skills would be a good fit. I handled two secretarial/clerical jobs right out of college and learned how to get work out the door and meet deadlines. I used Lotus and WordPerfect in those jobs. I also put in some time working in restaurants, where I learned how to handle stressful situations and smooth over ruffled feathers. I think all of these previous experiences will help me be a real team member in a law firm with the skills to handle indexing, document preparation, and whatever needs to be done. My internship experience in a small general practice helped me get a real understanding of how a busy law office works. I am not afraid to work hard and put in long hours, if needed. I believe my recent paralegal schooling gives me the basic concepts I need to continue this educational process and make a real contribution to your firm.

 **The bio is your story with your background, education, experience, skills, and personal qualities. It is the answer to many questions, the most likely being, "Tell me about yourself."** What lawyer goes to trial and leaves out the three key "smoking gun" documents that constitute the backbone of the case? None who wish to stay in practice! Now ask yourself: What paralegal applicant goes to an interview and leaves out the key valuable skills that will cause a compelling hiring decision to be made?

The bio serves another important function: If helps you know what you are *not* going to talk about as much as what you *will*. If you tend to be overly talkative when you get nervous, a strongly structured bio may help you curb your tongue. Paralegal applicants who let their "mouths run" often stray into disqualification territory.

By now the reasons to prepare a bio should be clear: It is a positive instrument in the hands of the interviewee. Its benefits include:

1.  It helps remind you not to go into territory that you do not want to talk about.
2.  It cuts down on nervousness and self-doubt.
3.  It gives you an anchor to return to if things go blank.
4.  It is a natural closer, if you did not get to discuss all aspects during your interview.
5.  It keeps you focused on the key message of why you are qualified for the position.
6.  It contains the answers to many "trick questions," global questions, overly general questions, and observations about you.

## The elements of the bio

When you prepare your bio, you should think about what you will emphasize, deemphasize, just touch on, or paint with specific detail.

The personal notes that follow were prepared in anticipation of a key interview. Use the inherent principles to guide your own planning.

1.  I am *not* going to talk for five minutes about the "lost" part of my youth, because it does not sell any skills.
2.  I *am* going to spend 30 seconds talking about my editor job because that goes to detail orientation.
3.  I am going to talk very *little* about my eight years of counseling, because this is a litigation job with 100,000 documents.
4.  When I mention any job, I will come up with *at least* one skill to describe.
5.  Each skill I describe will be transferable to the area of law.
6.  I will not stray onto personal territory I might be tempted to cover, because I realize it does not pertain to the legal market.

7. I will find a way to introduce some positive personal qualities without putting people off. The personal qualities will have to do with *perceived value in the eyes of the law firm.*

As you prepare your bio, you should hope for a positive reaction from yourself! Hopefully, you will be able to say, "You know, this sounds pretty darned good. *I* would hire me!" Believe your own bio! It should not be overblown, but it should be positive. The interview is not a time for understatement or subtlety. In the world of the interview, the self-effacing have little extra advantage.

---

# CONSTRUCTING
# A
# BIO

---

### 1. EDUCATION

### 2. PARALEGAL EDUCATION

### 3. INTERNSHIP OR RELEVANT PAST JOB

### *4. JOB SKILLS*

### 5. PERSONAL QUALITIES

---

## Two purposes for the interview process

Once you are ready to present yourself, you must remember the two purposes of the interview process:

1. To find the person they are going to hire (fall in love with) (build a family feeling for) (generate strong fervency of interest). This is the *qualification mechanism.* There is an urge to support an emotional/objective decision with enthusiasm. This enthusiasm is the basis for inviting the new person into the fold. It is a very natural process that occurs in every interview. *There is an urge to qualify and it has a snowball effect.*
2. There is a mandate to eliminate all the people who interview but one. This is just arithmetic; if they interview five they will get rid of four. That is the overall message. Maybe one interviewer only

recommends, or grades, or designates favorites, but the process is designed to disqualify everybody except one.

Therefore, every interviewer is under two mandates: fall in love with one and get rid of the rest. To counter these mandates, you must do what you can to avoid outright disqualification and build an enthusiastic, *positive bond* between you and the interviewer. Yes, interviews can be vexing experiences, but all the while you should be attempting to create a "fervency of interest" that has everything to do with the "blind date" (subtext) aspect of the interview. You must ascend from being a piece of paper to being a person, having a persona, being a friend.

1)  Stay Alive
2)  Keep Building Bonds and Fervency of Interest

## Assessing the intent of questions

We have already considered how a feeling of comfort and ease can be hazardous to your interviewing health. **As you go through an interview, you should consciously be assessing the intent of questions.** Questions that sound picky, trite, or clichéd may have a hard-to-discern purpose; they are meant to reveal poise, values, mettle under pressure, maturity, or some other quality an interviewer may be seeking. For example, "Are you planning on going to law school?" does not mean "You look so bright, will you be staying with us after you become a lawyer?" It means, "If we hire you, will you be leaving us soon?"

If a question makes you stop and think, maybe the question is designed to make you stop and think. Do not be afraid of a pregnant pause. Many interviewees are afraid of "dead air time." Even though time seems to slow down in these situations, there is no need to fume, sweat, huff, or hyperventilate. Pause. Ask for time to consider the question and do your best at answering the question. Maybe a long pause and thoughtful consideration is what they are looking for. After all, paralegals should not be impulsive.

Some questions are designed to reveal values and ethics. Be aware that hypotheticals and awkwardly posed questions may sound artificial, but they also may have an underlying purpose. One person put it this way: "If I could know people for two weeks, I would know for sure whether I would want to hire them. But I don't have two weeks, so I try to put people through questions and hypotheticals that will give me more information than I could possibly have in a normal 20-minute encounter."

This explains many of the perplexities of the interview. This is not benign torture; these are not perverse employers getting secret pleasure putting guinea pigs through a treacherous course. The interview is simply an attempt to learn a lot in a very short period of time. The difference then is in method and style.

### *The money question*

Questions about compensation are likely to come up in even the first interview. Consider these basic points:

- Field initial questions about money with answers that sound flexible. If you have a hard number in your mind, sound reasonable in the beginning, or you will be dispatched before you get a chance to negotiate.
- If someone insists on pinning you down about the money question, use a *range*. Most money questions which come up before there is a strong fervency of interest are designed to eliminate and disqualify.
- Before you react negatively to a low salary number, consider the *entire* compensation package. Strongly consider all benefits.
- Consider all of the *intangibles* before rejecting an offer such as: commuting, rapid transit, bad neighborhoods, location, office atmosphere, your particular working space, your desk, sophistication of computers, and all other potential distinctions.
- If you have a counter-offer, then sleep on it and call them the next day.

## The Root Canal Interview

Sometimes interviews can go very badly! They feel like root canals. Any interview can descend into a quagmire of dullness, hurt feelings, or tension. The professional paralegal must remember just to go through it patiently. Be as polite as possible. *Do not burn bridges.* Remember, lawyers talk to each other. Word gets around. *Contacts have power.* As much as you may want to say something insulting, speak your mind at an inappropriate time, or just let go with an entirely called-for remark, you must remain professional. Do whatever it takes to detach yourself from the feelings of a Root Canal Interview. Do not wear your feelings on your sleeve, and stay positive. If you can tell by someone's body language or posture or manner that you have said something that has you in trouble, stop talking about that. Go back to your bio and your skills; do what you can to correct a potentially damaging situation. If you can sense you are not going to be called back and this is a lost cause, stay ever composed. Shake hands and smile politely, observing the amenities that rule our civilized world.

## What you can learn from root canal interviews

First of all, do not punish yourself. Ask yourself if there is something basically wrong with your presentation (the text) or your manner (the subtext). If there is, work on it; if not, forget it. Sinking into a morass of negative self-blame is the most defeating thing you can do. If you do not have the right attitude, you have nothing. Nothing is worse than stopping a positive job search and productive interview just because you are taking two weeks to get over a depression. *Time is money* in the job search, and you never know which minute or hour is going to pay off.

If you have bad chemistry more than infrequently, maybe you should sit down and do some self-analysis. Ask yourself:

+ "Am I letting too much of my personality 'hang out' in the interview?"
+ "Is there something basic about my body language or attitude that might be causing these situations?"
+ "Am I so muted or distant that I am not allowing an enthusiastic bond to develop?"

## Do's and Don'ts of the Legal Interview

The following list will help you review key do's and don'ts before each interview:

1. Do prepare for the specific interview as much as you can.
2. Do not be late. Know the location.
3. Practice getting *up* for each interview.
4. Do not let temporary moodiness cast a noticeable pall over your interview.
5. Do not let a slip or flub distract you.
6. Do not ever say anything negative in the interview about anybody! Frame every response into a professionally considered, laudatory statement.
7. Conclude every interview positively, no matter how you feel.
8. Do not vent unreleased feelings about past employers.
9. Do not judge the firm by the personality of the interviewer. You may not have to work with that person much, or at all.

10. The interview begins and ends at the front door of the office. Do not apply make-up just before you go into the "inner sanctum." Do not give a muted cheer upon leaving the "inner sanctum." Secretaries and other support personnel are quietly observing you all the time.

## The Interview as Adventure

The interview is an adventure that you can embrace with excitement, anticipation, and expectation. It is like taking a ride on a roller coaster or a white-water river. Try to relish this experience. This attitude can be intoxicating. It helps you conquer the nerves and paralysis of preinterview preparation.

Interviews are tough, but you can lighten your step and brighten your eyes with this step-by-step internal dialogue.

1. The interview is an adventure because every interview is a totally unique event that will never be repeated in exactly the same way. It is *exciting* because it is unique and new to you.
2. The interview is an adventure because the interviewer cannot take away anything from you that you do not yet have. *They have no power over you, yet.*
3. The interview is an adventure because it just might change your life! Think back in your life to the turning points. There are probably two or three key interviews that absolutely changed it. That is an exciting thought. If you take that thought into each interview, you will have the knack of gaining this adventurous state of mind.

Approach the interview as adventure and you will enjoy some significant benefits:

a. You will be more enthusiastic.
b. Your mind will be clearer.
c. You will be less rigid and more fluid.
d. The "best you" will come out more easily.
e. You will exude vitality.
f. You will be perceived as having more *value.*

When you see the interview as an adventure, the preinterview dread does not put a drag on your performance. Then you can communicate competence, professional adaptability, and a personal dimension. This creates a bonding, a fervency of interest, and that distinction makes the hiring decision go your way.

## Summary

The interview is a potential minefield, but everyone wants an interview to go well. The interview can feel like a root canal. The interview is tense because very important life-changing decisions are being considered in a compact period of time in which so much is artificial and contrived. It is absolutely predictable that such a situation should be fraught with drama and tension.

A professional paralegal is working within a restricted world. This is no game, and there are a limited number of jobs in this world. When one considers the number of applicants and the number of advertised jobs as opposed to unadvertised leads, the message comes ringing through!

Prepare. Be at your best. Talk about the skills you have developed. Present yourself in the most positive and enthusiastic way.


The Interview is like Figure Skating . . .
You are in Competition,
But You Are All Alone On The Ice.

If You Do Poorly,
It Hardly Matters
What Your Competition Did.

If You Do Well,
You Can Do Nothing More.

# CHAPTER 5

## Getting Attention with Your Paralegal Resume

### What Is the Purpose of a Resume?

Opening a lecture with a question like this has an arresting quality. I waited for a response as classmates looked around at each other. Finally, wanting to end the silence, a few volunteered some responses.

"To get a job," said one. "To get hired," posed another. "To get work so I can pay my school loans." This got a laugh.

"The purpose of a resume is to get an interview!," I declared. "And when you understand that, you will understand virtually every rule and guiding principle regarding resumes."

These typical responses reveal a common misunderstanding concerning the resume and its purpose. It's not hard to understand, but many do not think about it. When someone is impressed with your resume, they do not hire you sight unseen—they call you in for an interview.

This should lead us to think about the overall "look" of the resume. *The resume must first draw interest before it can impress.* Drawing up a resume is a perceptual challenge! The initial impression of the resume, upon a three-second scan, is extremely important. If you try to impress with overlong descriptions and unnecessary and redundant elements, creating dense text without "white space," you risk losing your reader's interest before there *is* interest. So let's understand these two basic concepts:

- ◆ Your resume must be interesting before it can be impressive.
- ◆ Your resume should be crafted to get an interview.

If you are looking for an interview, then the resume need not "tell everything." It is allowed to be intriguing. Those who want to include too much are missing a real point. If you tell everything, but in doing so make it hard to read, you are defeating your purposes. Think of the resume as an advertisement (The Madison Avenue Rule). Why? Today's resume must attain a high basic quality and be edited and crafted visually so that it will gain immediate attention. It cannot be a document that is hard on the eyes, exhaustive, thorough, yet accurate. If that were ever permissible at any time in the past, it certainly isn't now in the more competitive job market. All of these factors derive from a rule that sums up these challenges all at once—*The 30-Second Rule*!

## The 30-Second Rule—"Love at First Glance"

The 30-Second Rule can be stated as follows: **The first time anyone reads your resume they will probably give it no longer than 30 seconds.** That is not long to make a positive impression. A quick cursory look is what every resume gets the first time around. An impression is made; the reader puts it in one of maybe three probable stacks (Interested, Maybe, Absolutely Not) or, even worse, two stacks (Maybe and No). Consider today's "short-attention-span" American culture and the pace of professional life. It will confirm that you have a very short amount of time within which to create a good impression.

The challenge in writing a resume is that you must sum up your professional life, initially, in 30 seconds. Once you get someone's attention, then of course, they read it over more thoroughly. But if you score negatively in the first 30 seconds, you are in trouble. Imagine a hiring manager sitting at his or her desk reading resumes. The mahogany desk is covered with pieces of paper in various shades of off-white, gray, beige, light yellows, or pale blues. Your resume is in this group. The first impressions your resume makes are *visual* and *tactile*. High-quality paper with a well-chosen color are the first mandates.

Since the legal profession is conservative, serious-minded, and intense (see Chapter Four), flashy and shocking colors and graphic techniques should be avoided. Yes, there is room for individuality, but only within conservative parameters. If you employ blue, green, brown, or red, make the color *very close to white.* In some fields, an eye-catching color can be an advantage; in the legal field, it is considered unprofessional. Choose the highest quality paper you feel you can afford, and select an attractive and legible typeface (font). You may need to adjust the font's point size and the space between lines of text so that your resume fits on one page. These will create the overall look that governs the initial impression of the reader.

After briefly checking the color and texture, the eyes go over the resume as a whole. *White space* becomes very important. Anyone who has had training in marketing or advertising has learned that the eye needs rest and will move toward white space. If the document makes the reader squint and furrow the brow to get into it, rather than letting the reader's eye flow easily from one section to the next, then the "graphic look" of this all-important document has been neglected. Billions of dollars are spent on advertising—don't ignore those lessons. The level of competition in the professional paralegal marketplace dictates that you approach your resume in this way. We are creatures who respond to subtle visual cues and impressions all day long. That many of these elements of modern life escape our conscious awareness is a testament to their power and influence.

> That which affects you subconsciously,
> Can be just as powerful
> As that which affects you consciously.

The following elements are employed in creating an effective resume:

- paper quality (Bond, Linen)
- paper color
- choice of font (style)
- choice of point size
- layout
- white space
- use of graphics (bullets, lines)
- printer (commercial or laser quality)
- ink (some inks smudge on certain kinds of paper)

Before we discuss how the 30-Second Rule influences design and content, proper attention should be paid to the above basic elements. Many people are aware of these required state-of-the-art standards and yet think they can take short cuts. Those who grab a ream of copy paper and grind out 50 resumes on a photocopy machine are truly missing the boat.

Remember, the people reading your resume have handled *hundreds* of others. They have minimum standards.

### Editorial content and style

The 30-Second Rule has many repercussions. Editorial content and style are affected by the basic mission: Get your message across in a *visually appealing manner* with a *highly readable and fast-paced style.* Because of the 30-Second Rule, you must write in a style that moves the eye along quickly. *Past tense verbs* should begin sentences. Avoid the use of the word "I" and formal sentence construction.

| | |
|---|---|
| *Don't say:* | " . . . I was given a promotion after two years in the Shipping Department. I received awards for productivity and punctuality and eventually I was made Supervisor . . . " |
| *Instead say:* | " . . . Promoted to Shipping Department Supervisor after receiving awards for productivity and punctuality over a two-year period . . . " |

Beginning your sentences with a past-tense power verb (the "I" is understood) immediately shortens the phrase and gets to the point. The power verb forces you to be specific and keeps the style *dynamic.* **The modern state-of-the-art resume should be pointed, direct, and substantive.** If you find yourself explaining a lot and saying little, check your construction. Are you using the "past-tense, power verb construction"?

### The kiss of death

Perhaps we should pause amidst the talk of style and format and talk about the kiss of death—spelling and other grammatical errors. The most attractive, well-written resume, hailing the virtues of the most qualified paralegal, can fail the applicant if it contains a spelling error. **Typos and other errors get you disqualified. The solution is to proofread, get others to proofread, and then proofread again.**

Remember also to *check your address and phone number.* One gentleman with 15 years of experience could not get an interview to "save his life." We wondered why until I got a phone call from one of my attorney friends. The conversation was rather abrupt. "If Mr. *X* is wondering why he isn't getting any interviews, tell him the phone number he has on his resume is not his!" This is a typo that won't get you disqualified, but it won't get you called, either.

## The One-Page Rule

Certainly there is room for individual style; distinctive resumes that have a special flare are highly desirable within limits of acceptability. However, there is a quick-moving, to-the-point quality about all effective resumes, which is forced upon us by the One-Page Rule. The One-Page Rule, which grows logically from the 30-Second Rule, is simply, "Keep the resume from going over one page in length."

"I have done too much in my life to contain it on one page," protested one student. To which I responded: "The President of the United States could have a one-page resume!"

A well-written, highly edited resume goes through several phases. At its best, a resume is analyzed word by word. Each word should be essential to the particular description and the whole image. Is there another word that would fit better? Is this phrase too long? Could these two phrases be blended? Does that detail need to be in at all? Am I missing a crucial element to this description? Do all of these descriptions work to picture me as a viable paralegal candidate? As you go through this process, you will discover that your resume will likely get shorter.  **Many two-page resumes are simply *overwritten*.** They labor too long on past experiences that are only mildly relevant. Four-line descriptions can often be reduced to one. Some two-page resumes make too much use of white space and margins and thus waste space. Many techniques can be used to take the air out of two-page resumes. It is all a matter of editing to focus and bring out the key points. The sheer act of having to condense your background to one page automatically accomplishes for people what they could not have done without that discipline. The One-Page Rule is an automatic editor: Keep to it and you will see how quickly you develop the clarity and focus you need.

## The 10-Year Rule and the Short/Long Rule

To fit in with the mandates of the 30-Second Rule and the One-Page Rule, the 10-Year Rule and the Short/Long Rule must exist. For the older paralegal applicant who has been in the working world for longer than 10 years, take heart in the fact that you are under no special hidden requirement to cover more than the most recent 10 years. Some want to reach back farther than 10 years to include some meaningful past experience,

**Fig. 5-1**

Sarah M. Kennedy

4965 Cold Creek Rd.
Hudson, New York                                    (Phone)

EMPLOYMENT OBJECTIVE: A challenging position in a Juvenile/Family Law practice

EDUCATION:

Hudson River Community College. Schenectady, New York. December, 1994. Curriculum included concentrated course work in Basic Legal Concepts, Legal Research, Litigation, Real Property, and Family Law.

Montessori Education Center of Upper State New York. Schenectady, New York. July, 1991.

Montessori Certification for Infants to Toddlers (birth to 36 months). Emphasis placed on Child Development, Environment Management, and Administration.

Pennsylvania State University. University Park, Pennsylvania. May, 1990. Bachelor of Science in Psychology, including coursework in Statistics, Child and Adolescent Psychology, and Psychological Testing. Gamma Phi Alpha, Chapter Beta Delta.

SPECIAL SKILLS:

| | | | |
|---|---|---|---|
| * | WordPerfect 6.0 | * | Communication Techniques |
| * | WestLaw | * | Legal Research Assignments |
| * | Drafting and Editing | * | Sign Language |
| * | Spanish | * | Interpersonal Skills |

PROFESSIONAL EXPERIENCE:

Head Director. Setting up and managing an environment, speaking on child development, counseling, and parent/teacher conferences.

Assistant Director. Assisting head director in her duties. Assuming charge when head director is absent. Planning and preparing schedules; setting up and creating special environments.

EMPLOYMENT HISTORY:

Montessori School                    Assistant Intern/Assistant
Schenectady, New York                Director/Head Director
                                     September, 1989 to Present

but general reaction will be: "If you have to go back that far, is it really relevant experience?"

The Short/Long Rule is a corollary to the 10-Year Rule. Try to get at least three jobs on your resume (try not to fall *short* of that), but you need not go any *longer* than six jobs. There are obvious exceptional circumstances which might dictate violating these guidelines, but if you have only one page to work with, it is not advisable to go longer than six jobs for sheer lack of space. If you have fewer than three jobs, you certainly cannot invent past employment. However, there are volunteer experiences and educational endeavors which can add weight to the resume of a young person. See Figure 5-1, the Sarah M. Kennedy Resume.

## The *FAB* Paralegal Resume Filter

The 30-Second Rule and the competitive market dictate that your state-of-the-art resume be FAB. FAB stands for:

1) **Features**
2) **Advantages**
3) **Benefits**

The term is borrowed from sales and marketing. If you were marketing a commodity or service, you would describe its characteristics, talk about the natural advantages that would come from its use, and describe the subsequent impact that it would have on someone's life—how it would *improve* another's life. This filter through which all potential resume material passes should be used when deciding if an element from your education (such as "sorority involvement") is worth more than something from an earlier job involving "balancing books and basic accounting."

For example, the FAB paralegal resume filter will tell you that if you have only two lines available on your resume, and you are choosing from sorority membership or a job that you could expand upon with accounting skills, then there would be no question. The FAB formula says that sorority involvement may be a *feature*, but it has little *advantage* and *benefit* to the potential employer. The book balancing and accounting work is a very transferable skill and holds great potential *benefit* to the firm/legal setting (employer).

### Features

Your mission in writing a resume is to decide exactly what about your background you want to include and what you will deemphasize (or not include at all). Once you have decided this, you have established the *features*. Some people find it helpful to obtain counsel from a job placement advisor about their background. The challenge in selecting your features is described in the above example, namely, choosing between *emotional or sentimental attachment* to a part of our lives and education or work background that provides *transferable and professionally valuable experiences*. You must become dispassionate about the features on your resume.

One female graduate from 1986 had 10 years experience counseling the disabled, along with five years of proofreading work. Knowing that the editing experience offered much transferable material that could be advantageous to a potential employer, she deemphasized the counseling and only devoted a single line in her resume to this part of her life, while devoting five lines to the editing experience. This is where the honing and creativity come into play. A *feature* might be difficult to omit, but the question becomes: How do we treat that feature to draw out *advantage* and *benefit*?

Once you have determined exactly what elements are going to be included in your resume and how much space you are going to give each element, then you need to determine layout and placement. The 30-Second Rule looms large at this point in determining what comes first, at the top of the resume. Another corollary of the 30-Second Rule will help: the "Sell the Sizzle, Then the Steak" Rule.

A winning approach to layout and design is to put the most prominent paralegal qualifiers at the top of your resume. As the resume proceeds, those elements that are substantial, but not as eye-catching, are included ("the steak"). If you have chosen your features well, there will be few irrelevant or unimportant elements on your resume. Still, you must determine—which comes first? What comes next? What goes last? Summations, Listings, Profiles, Summaries of Qualifications, and Special Skills are all essentially snapshots of your skills and background that should go on the top- to middle-third of your resume. If you are going to employ any kind of summation section, then it should go toward the top.  **The theory behind the "Sell the Sizzle, Not the Steak" Rule is that you are putting the most appealing and instantly comprehensible and persuasive elements of your background at the top-third of the resume.** The most persuasive elements will probably include:

**Technical/Computer Skills.** This is the Computer Age, and everything from typing skills to kinds of software and hardware need to be prominently displayed in the top-third of your resume. These skills can be listed in a visually appealing way and don't take up too much space. They are ideal for the top half of the resume.

**Paralegal Education.**    Unless you have some kind of previous legal experience that is more important than your paralegal education, the paralegal training you have received should be prominently displayed at the top third also. We'll go into more detail concerning how to present your educational background on the resume later in this chapter.

**"Snapshots" of Your Background.**    In the next chapter, you will find a list of paralegal buzz words that are powerful to include in resumes. Check the examples of resumes contained in this chapter. They summarize skills and qualifications in meaningful and persuasive ways. They "sizzle" merely because they are summed up or listed. Snapshots of your background give a quick visual readout of *who you think you are.* For example, "computer literate paralegal with strong customer service and business background seeks a position in a busy bankruptcy practice."

**Strongly Related Experiences.**    Strongly related experiences such as legal internships, work with legislatures as a volunteer, or activity allied to legal should all be worked into the top third of the resume. It is advisable to create a "Legal Experience" section if it is substantial enough to warrant such treatment.

## Advantages

When it comes to describing your features as advantages, you must think like the person reading your resume. We are after advantages described for the reader, not the writer. The natural resume written as a chronological document without any concern for a paralegal placement will emphasize only titles. **Do *not* talk only about your past *titles*; talk about your *skills.*** Supervisor, Manager, Administrator, Assistant Manager, Director, Vice President—these are used in descriptions of past experiences. If you only describe these features without mentioning the skills needed to attain these positions, you are not describing your background with the needed advantages. In creating your resume, remember to:

1) Avoid pushing titles, unless the job for which you are applying calls for exactly the same kinds of experience.
2) Elaborate on the skills that you developed in order to get promoted. These skills are the important advantages. Sometimes it is easy to forget the basic responsibilities that we grew into.

3) Pull out skills from past experience and frame them in the form of an advantage and benefit to the attorney.

Here's an example of a basic description:

> Joe's Bar and Grill, Bartender and Supervisor: Hired waitresses and waiters, served drinks, maintained schedules, acted as bouncer.

This is an elaborated description:

> Joe's Bar and Grill, Manager: Balanced books, made bank deposits, controlled and monitored inventory, dealt with outside vendors and developed strong interpersonal skills in occasionally stressful situations.

This is the kind of skill analysis that many people fail to do when creating their resume. They may say to themselves, "It was just a bartender job!" Instead, you need to realize how many varied organizational skills you have developed and how many interpersonal experiences went into your growth and maturity.

## *Benefits*

Skill analysis is invaluable to the effective paralegal job search. The people who have done this necessary work can, after a thoughtful pause, deliver a one-to-two minute description of their transferable skills. The answer to the question, "Why would you make a good paralegal?," is answered by the person who has worked through this self-analysis so that they can deliver an effective sales pitch.

The benefit that you bring to an employer in many cases is implicit. "Organizational Skills" is a common skill with an immediate connection for an attorney. You may need to elaborate on how you built those skills in order to demonstrate that you can handle the pressure and tension that might have come along with your organizational tasks. Many people claim to have this skill, so the challenge is to stand out when you describe "organizational skills."

Some other skills and advantages are less implicit. In these cases, it is incumbent upon you to truly show how that skill is a benefit in a legal setting or law office environment. For example, an editorial background shows that a paralegal applicant has a keen eye for detail and can keep things from falling through the cracks. A restaurant background shows that a paralegal applicant can handle high stress and deal with demanding situations. It is this kind of transferring that you need to do for the resume (and interview) phase of the effective paralegal job search.

## Self analysis and skill transference

Below, we will discuss how you can analyze your skills and present them as benefits to your potential employer.

A paralegal applicant with five past jobs is faced with a genuine challenge in writing a resume; in fact, with concentration, this exercise can be accomplished fundamentally in 15 minutes. The first task is just to analyze all the activities that were involved in each job. As an example, a restaurant background, though seemingly simple, is actually multifaceted. There is the public component, the memory component, physical activity, inventory, balancing, handling numbers and orders, dealing with vendors, handling irate customers, and the developing of diplomatic and personable qualities. A job can be broken down in terms of activities, which in turn evolve into skills. Then, a benefit can be highlighted for the attorney: "This is a hard working person who can handle stress and won't fly off the handle the first time things get tense."

Grouping activities and skills occurs naturally as you analyze activities and skills from the different jobs. To help you with this task, take 15 minutes and do the following: describe all of your past employment and experience on the basis of the raw descriptions. After describing them, analyze them for skills and group them. Create a picture of the image that is developing. Emphasize skills and talents that would be particularly beneficial to a legal office or setting. As you do this, you will discover a picture of yourself that you might not have perceived before.

This process can be enlightening. After this kind of exercise, you will conclude that you have a viability you might not have realized before in quite the same way. This exercise not only helps you with your skill analysis, but it also helps you with your self-image. Most of us need to stop minimizing ourselves.

## Parts of the Resume

In this section we will explore the various parts of a resume: Education, Professional or Work Experience, Skill Assessment Sections (Profiles and Objectives), Special/Technical sections. While these do not cover all possible titles you might assign to parts of your resume, they do cover the territory in terms of topics.

You will note that we did not mention a Personal section, which would describe your personal interests and hobbies. Resumes used to routinely include a personal section in the 1970s and before, but a

Personal section is no longer considered germane to the hiring process. Including such information may make you seem out of touch.

## *Education*

An entry paralegal should include formal paralegal training at or near the top of the resume. Following your paralegal training, in reverse chronological order, insert your other educational experiences. Include four-year degrees, associate degrees, certificates, seminars, or programs attended. No matter how you lead (whether with the degree, the school, or the date), make sure it is a consistent presentation that includes the following information: school, city, state, date, degrees or level attained, kind of program, curriculum description.

Please refer back to Figure 5-1, Sarah Kennedy Resume, at page 92. In this resume, the education section is a full one-third of the page because the paralegal is young and lacks a long work history. She has fully described not only her paralegal curriculum, but also a special educational qualification (Child Development), followed by her substantial four-year degree program. Note that she has described her education in such a full and detailed way because all of it relates to the practice area she is seeking. Her Employment Objective is a "challenging career in a Juvenile/Family Law practice." In this case she is not only establishing her educational credentials in general, but she is also making a case for being a well-trained entry juvenile/family law paralegal. She is definitely putting the "sizzle" at the top by following her Education with a Special Skills section.

If you are older and have quite a bit of educational and professional experience, you may want to treat some older educational background lightly or not at all. Some people who have bachelor's degrees simply leave off an older associate's degree to make room for something else they deem more important. You need not put *every* certificate gained or seminar attended, if they go back too far or have questionable benefit to you.

If you do not want to emphasize previous educational experience by placing it at the top of the resume (for example, if you have an incomplete degree or a degree that does not seem relevant to the paralegal position), there is the technique of separating your "Legal Education" from your "Previous Education." This is highly subjective and may not be a problem to some. But truly, "One man's sizzle is another man's fizzle." Please note the next resume (Figure 5-2 Aaron G. Friedland Resume) in which the paralegal training is blended in with the legal experience at the top, and the previous experience is put together with previous education.

**Fig. 5-2**

Aaron G. Friedland
12456 Miami Boulevard
Miami, Florida
(Phone)

LEGAL EDUCATION AND EXPERIENCE

<u>Institute of Paralegal Studies.</u> Tallahassee, Florida.
Courses concentrated on Basic Legal Concepts, Research and
Writing, Business Organizations, Litigation, and an
extensive practical internship as a requirement. Completed
December 1993.

<u>Warren B. Reem, Attorney at Law.</u> Miami, Florida. Estate
Administration specialist. October 1993 to present.
Paralegal.
Drafted pleadings and motions, conducted client interviews.

<u>Kerry S. Lada, Attorney at Law, P.C.,</u> Tallahassee, Florida,
August 1993 to December 1993. Paralegal Internship.
Assisted in trial notebook preparation and client interviews.
Researched a variety of assigned issues on matters coming up
for trial.
Drafted demand letters and motions.
Performed a wide variety of office functions and assigned
tasks.

RELATED QUALIFICATIONS AND SKILLS

Extensive client contact. Extensive experience with computer
applications. Training in WestLaw and Lexis.

BUSINESS EDUCATION AND EXPERIENCE

<u>Primary Total Systems, Inc.</u> Tallahassee, Florida.
Customer Service—4/92 to 2/93

<u>Foundation Information Technologies.</u> Miami, Florida. 2/85 to
9/91
Conversion Analyst—7/88 to 9/91
Account Executive—8/87 to 7/88
Account Representative—2/85 to 8/87

<u>American National Bank.</u> Miami, Florida.
Chief Cashier—2/83 to 1/85

<u>Citizens National Bank.</u> Miami, Florida, 9/80 to 2/83
Teller Supervisor—8/82 to 2/83
Proof Operator—9/81 to 8/82
Bookkeeping Clerk—9/80 to 9/81

<u>Southern Florida Junior College.</u> Miami, Florida. June 1984.
A.R.S. in Accounting

*A Word About Omitting Dates:* Often people are trying to hide their age when they omit dates. However, omissions will be noticeable and bring people's attention to the spot that the applicant is ostensibly attempting to conceal. This is not to say that you are committing an unpardonable sin by omitting a date on an early educational experience, but at the same time, one should consider the irony that someone, upon viewing the absence of a date, just might assume you are older than you are!

## Professional or work experience

### The Hard Chronology

You must add a "Hard Chronology" somewhere to your resume. A resume without dates and job listings is not recommended. There should be a part of your resume in which a mildly interested person can discover the basics of your background. The entry should contain at least these elements — your hard chronology:

Company
Title
City
State
Date
Description

The way these elements are handled should be consistent with all of the employment experiences listed. In the following example, the job title comes before the company:

Manager, Sam's Barbecue Heaven; Terre Haute, IN, 1991-1993

This is preferable to:

Sam's Barbecue Heaven, Manager; Terre Haute, IN, 1991-1993

On the other hand . . .

IBM, Delivery Driver; Chicago, IL, 1992-

is probably better than . . .

Delivery Driver, IBM; Chicago, IL, 1992-

**Lead with the most impressive, substantial element first and then follow with the less imposing element.** Please refer again to the resume of Aaron Friedland. This individual was leading with his computer and wordprocessing systems experience. He described certain jobs in great detail and fully embellished them to show a level of responsibility and technical skill. The customer service and account executive positions he only listed, figuring that the nature of those jobs was self-evident and less significant than his technical background.

Beware of redundancy and repetition! One of the most common mistakes made in the work experience section is to mindlessly describe the same type of job three or four different times. This is stupefying, unless it relates directly to the job you are seeking. If you have jobs that are basically the same, take advantage of that and line the jobs up and describe them with one short paragraph. In this situation, you may want to make more of your education or special skills; use white space artfully and make the look more appealing. The worst thing you can do is make the descriptions dense, repetitive, and crowded.

### Gaps and Other Problems

If you have potential problems in your background, such as gaps or jobs that you do not wish to draw attention to, then grapple with these issues in the "hard chronology." Each should be dealt with independently so that different approaches can be utilized. Some choose to avoid explanation. This approach lets the interviewer "discover" the gap or other problem. Some choose to cover the period with volunteer experience or part-time jobs or a combination of such. After assisting with the creation of thousands of resumes, I recommend that these problems be dealt with creatively and with a number of different approaches. Each person must assess these questions:

1) How big is this gap? How bad is it, really?
2) Am I just overly sensitive about this period?
3) Can it be subordinated for the purposes of the resume? Will this hurt my chances of getting an interview?
4) Will I be able to feel comfortable with this explanation in my interview?
5) When I explain this in the interview, will it soothe doubts or create suspicion?

Fig. 5-3

Don Tollefson
1135 Fair Oaks Drive
Pasadena, California
(Phone)

## OBJECTIVE

Seeking an internship and potential employment position as a paralegal in a challenging environment that provides exposure to many areas of the law.

## EDUCATION

**San Gabriel Valley Paralegal Studies**, Pasadena, California—Enrolled in program for Paralegal Studies. Will graduate in January, 1995.

**University of California at Berkeley**, Berkeley, California—Began work on a Master of Arts degree in Theater. Accumulated approximately 40 credit-hours. 1990.

**University of California at Berkeley**, Berkeley, California—Bachelor of Fine Arts in Theater. Originally pursued a major in Linguistics and Theater, but then switched to the specialized B.F.A. Theater degree program. 1989.

## SKILLS

**Paralegal Training:** Classes to date have covered legal research, litigation, business organizations, torts, real estate law. Dissolution and investigations to follow.

**Client Relations:** Extensive background in the theater is excellent preparation for dealing with interpersonal situations. Can make people feel at ease.

**Computer Use and Knowledge:** Exposed to computers since 1980. Primary experience is on MS-DOS systems, also with Windows and Macintosh.

**Software Familiarity:** Wordstar, WordPerfect, Microsoft Word, spreadsheets, and database management packages.

## EMPLOYMENT

Self-employed as an actor and light choreographer from June 1989 to present.
**Off The Edge Productions:** Glendale, California—Instructor and actor June 1990 to present.
**Perkins Restaurant:** Burbank, California—Waiter from June 1992 to February 1993.
**Le Peep Restaurant:** Pasadena, California—Waiter from July 1989 to August 1990.

## REFERENCES    Available upon request.

In every case of doubt or question, consult a counselor or knowledge-able friend for advice. The two crucial questions are: Will this keep me from getting an interview? When I get the interview, will this explanation help me?

## The skill assessment section

Figure 5-3, Don Tollefson Resume, shows you that there is a way of summing yourself up that transcends the "hard chronology." This is true of everyone, especially those of us who are younger. Your skills, talents, and qualifications constitute much more of what you are at the age of 24 than does your work experience. This is the reason for the Skill Assessment/Summary of Qualifications section. Regardless of our age, we are more qualified than we look (or certainly feel we are). If it is not so in reality, it is certainly so from our own personal perspective. Therefore, most of us should labor at the creation of a section in our resume in which we sum up our talents, qualifications, or skills—*the resume within the resume*!

Note that Mr. Tollefson has been in the theater and worked in restaurants. He also discusses his self-employment. Now, pay attention to his Skills section. He covers "Paralegal Training," "Client Relations," "Computer Use and Knowledge," and "Software Familiarity." When an interested party reads this part of his resume, one discovers a much fuller elaboration of a person than would be expected from one who has just worked in theater and restaurants. If this applicant had not handled that elaboration with detail, color, and sophistication, he might have been relegated to paralegal unemployment. As it was, this paralegal described himself as a well-trained professional paralegal with an ease in dealing with many types of people and who could handle the busy congestion and activity of a law office with the commensurate demands of word-processing and other computer technology. This Skill Assessment section gives an interested employer a look at a full and complex individual who would probably be a wonderful asset to a law office. Without the Skill element, he could have been labeled with broad-brush characterizations that eliminated him from the interview.

Using the "Resume within a Resume," many paralegal applicants today sum themselves up quickly in a tightly written summation of experience that includes (besides a simple listing of skills) a kind of "biography" structure.

Fig. 5-4

Denton John Armistead
1213 Highway 242
Dallas, Texas 70332
(Phone)

# EDUCATION

**Texas Paralegal Institute.** Ft. Worth, Texas
Paralegal Certificate; September 1994.

**Virginia University.** Richmond, Virginia.
B.S. Wildlife Biology/Management; June 1984.

# LEGAL EXPERIENCE

**Cooper & Abramowitz.** Dallas, Texas.
Worked over 100 hours as paralegal intern with firm specializing in medical malpractice and insurance litigation. July-August, 1994.

# PROFESSIONAL SKILLS

In over 14 years of Business Management, have proven ability to:

- ◆ Worked efficiently in busy job environments by utilizing high energy, time management skills, and task prioritization
- ◆ Prepared budgets, P&L statements, and accounting reports
- ◆ Generated reports and documents via various computer systems

# PROFESSIONAL EXPERIENCE

**Operations Manager.** Avis Rent-A-Car, Wichita Falls, TX (10/89-12/93). Acted as operations manager in hiring, firing, training, and developing of 100 employees. Achieved highest Quality Assurance score in company. Developed new procedures that increased customer service and revenue.

**Senior Projects Manager.** Central Parking Systems, Kansas City, MO (3/87-8/89). Trained 50 employees, including management, clerical, supervisory, maintenance, valet, and cashier personnel. Streamlined operational methods that improved overall efficiency and employee morale.

**District Manager.** Econo Rent-A-Car, Dallas, TX (4/85-12/86)
Operated busy district with five offices as district manager. Reversed deficit in district within two months.

In Figure 5-4, Denton John Armistead Resume, the paralegal has summarized 14 years of business experience in a crisp visual style. He avoids boring the reader by summing up the most *vital* parts of the experience, rather than giving rote descriptions of jobs. This packages him attractively, showing that he knows he is moving into the paralegal world and he is purposefully moving from one domain into another. Without this kind of treatment, one might question whether the person truly understood the direction in which he was heading.

In Figure 5-5, Jane Nottingham Resume, the paralegal sums up her experience at the beginning of the resume with a "Profile." With this treatment, the paralegal applicant is declaring who she is and how she thinks she can contribute to a law office. This is a nondefensive approach to a strong professional background. The sense that is being conveyed is that this person made a deliberate, considered, and well-thought-out decision about a new career transition. Without this approach, the interested reader might wonder, "Is this person over-qualified and expecting too much?" "Will this person work in the world of law?" "How can a producer of the electronic media have any interest in the law?"

In the very beginning of the resume, she begins with the value that she is bringing to the law firm. She is declaring her skills before her work background. She is deflecting the focus away from her actual job descriptions (which have to do with TV stations and publishers) and "forcing" the attention of the reader on the qualities that she thinks she brings to the legal environment.

There are many examples of the treatment of skills, summations, and profiles in professional resumes today. It is easy enough to find an outstanding example or create a look that will satisfy you and take an important visual place in your resume. The appropriateness of a certain form or format for your particular resume is something about which you should seek advice and input. But the basic elements of a good skill assessment section, apart from its visual appeal, are important to consider.

1) Does it truly reflect your skills?
2) Is it easy to see how you developed your skills from reading the rest of your resume?
3) Are your skills valuable in a legal setting or law office?
4) Have you put your skills in the proper order? (most important to legal first, and then in descending order)
5) Will you be able to base a strong oral presentation—your bio—upon the Skills section and make it believable and compelling?

**Fig. 5-5**

Jane L. Nottingham
2100 North Avenue
Chicago, IL 60601
(Phone)

Profile
    Experienced with WP 6.0 and WestLaw Certified, mature
    professional capable of handling multiple assignments
    simultaneously. Performs well in deadline-sensitive
    environment. Works well independently and with others.
    Highly developed interpersonal skills. Experienced
    researcher. Versatile writer.

Education
    Northern Paralegal Institute, Chicago, Illinois; November
    1994. Paralegal Certificate. ABA-approved curriculum,
    including: Legal Research and Writing, Litigation,
    Business Organization, Real Property, Family Law, Estate
    Administration, and Ethics.

    College of St. Scholastica, Duluth, Minnesota. May 1990.
    Bachelor of Arts Degree in Communication (Writing
    Emphasis).

Legal Experience
    Office of the General Counsel, U.S.D.A., Chicago,
    Illinois.
    Paralegal Internship. September-November, 1994
    Litigation Support: Assisted in case file management;
    summarized depositions; prepared exhibits for briefs;
    researched and wrote a descriptive speech outline;
    researched in traditional law library settings.

Employment History
    KQDS AM/FM, Minneapolis, Minnesota; October 1990-October
    1992.
        Media Representative: Specialized in researching and
        developing a new client base. Served active community
        relations role.

    WABC AM/FM, Peoria, Illinois; October 1989-August 1990.
        Media Representative: Target marketed accounts for two
        distinct formats.

    Hammer and Smith Publishers, Chicago, Illinois; March
    1989-June 1989.
        Marketing Assistant: Researched markets of health and
        wellness literature users. Wrote technical marketing
        material.

    KKRR-TV, Gary, Indiana; September 1984-February 1989.
        Public Affairs Director: Analyzed needs of broadcast
        market. Created, wrote, and produced announcements and
        programs. Represented station's interests on
        committees and boards.

### The special/technical skills section

Many people are concerned with one element in a paralegal resume: They desire to make clear their complete qualifications with computers, hardware, and software. The devotion of one part of your resume to these skills is highly recommended. Please refer to Figure 5-6, Mirriam Dellahousay Resume, and see how this section is placed at the top of the resume so that even a mildly interested reader will note it.

A common error is to place this section too close to the bottom of the resume, thus risking that a hurried perusal would miss this vital part of your value package.

## When You're Qualified . . . You're Qualified!

Something must be said for the simple approach. Some people do well with resumes that are very *spare*. For example, those with previous medical qualifications often have a "free pass" into an interview situation. Their qualifications are in demand. The man revealed in Figure 5-7, Don Arnesson Resume, got entry employment soon after graduation and was rapidly advanced. (In fact, all of the people whose resumes are shown in this chapter got entry-level employment soon after graduation.) This man, however, took the "lean" approach and did not suffer for it. This is not to say that his next position might not require a different kind of approach.

This is a bare bones resume, but it is unmistakable in its statement that the applicant has a medical background. He did not clutter the resume because he knew that he would probably get an interview based solely upon his qualifications. This created a specific image. The image being communicated was one of maturity and qualification. It almost says, "Interview me and you'll see how qualified I am." Some people might have a problem with this resume, but the proof is in the pudding. He got a job at the first firm to which he applied, right after graduation.

## Targeted Resumes—More Than One!

The truly prepared paralegal about to engage in the effective paralegal job search will have the ability to "stylize" resumes. This is nothing more than taking a basic resume, which should be saved on a diskette, and making adjustments so that a differently targeted resume can be produced within a day.

Fig. 5-6

Mirriam Dellahousay
2000 Potomac Parkway
Fairfax, Virginia 21300
(Phone)

## LEGAL EXPERIENCE:

**Patriot Insurance Co.,** Richmond, Virginia; Legal Secretary/Paralegal—In House Attorney for Insurance Company. Maintained attorney's calendar, hearing and trial lists, tickler system, filing, deposition summaries. Emphasis in Workers' Compensation, products liability, and personal injury related cases. 8/91 to 8/92

**Burlingame, Burlingame and Smith,** Arlington, Virginia, Legal Secretary—Workers' Compensation Law. Dealt with clients, handled wordprocessing, and maintained files. Tickling and scheduling. 5/91 to 8/91

## COMPUTER SYSTEMS:

IBM PC Environment—WordPerfect 4.2, 5.0, 5.1,

Novel Netware system, Q&A, ORG Plus

Lexis and WestLaw

dBase III and IV and Lotus 1-2-3

Microsoft Word, Hypercard, Netway

EDUCATION:    1993—Virginia Community College—Associates Degree (Paralegal Program) Graduation 7/93

## PREVIOUS EXPERIENCE:

**Mellenkamps Bar and Grill,** Richmond, Virginia, Word Processor and Office Assistant. Worked for Owner/Manager, handled all duties regarding restaurant management, inventory, payroll, and vendor relations. 10/89 to 3/93

**The Aristocrat Restaurant,** Washington, DC; Accounting and Wordprocessing. Responsible for office management tasks and basic bookkeeping and accounting duties. Given responsibilities by manager of cash deposits and highly confidential financial and legal matters. Dealt with business vendors.

REFERENCES WILL BE FURNISHED UPON REQUEST

**Fig. 5-7**

Don Arnesson
300 E. Austin Street
Seattle, Washington
(Phone)


Education:

> Northwest Community College
> Seattle, Washington
> Paralegal Diploma—June, 1994
>
> Northwest Oregon School of Anesthesia
> Portland, Oregon
> 1974-1976
> Graduated, Certificate of Training
>
> University of Arkansas
> Monticello, Arkansas
> 1971-1973
> Graduated, Associate Degree of Nursing

Work Experience:

> April 1991-December 1992
> Food and Beverage Service
> Warwick Hotel
> Tacoma, Washington
>
> November 1983-April 1991
> Owner/Operator
> Professional Anesthesia Service
> Ulysses, Idaho
>
> June 1991-October 1983
> Anesthesiology, Inc.
> Staff Anesthetist
> Spokane, Washington
>
> April 1976-May 1981
> Staff Anesthetist
> St. Elizabeth's Hospital
> Paducah, Kentucky

References Available Upon Request

Start with a *Basic Paralegal Resume.*

Then, by employing an "Objective" at the beginning of the document, state something like: "Seeking a Paralegal Position in an Estates Administration and Probate Practice." This will lead you to a second resume that is only substantively different because it has a *targeted objective.*

Now you have an *Estate Administration Paralegal Resume.*

A third resume might be aimed at a nonlaw office environment. Who knows? There might be an advertised lead for a "Document Specialist" in a corporation of which you have never remotely heard. This might be the perfect time for a Nontraditional/Alternative Career Resume.

In this case, you might either bring your past experience to the top of the resume or redo your skills summary to reflect experience in a certain industry or service. Some might just redesign an "Objective" that states: "Seeking a Position in a Corporation Utilizing Legal Training and Business Background."

Some people have resumes for general situations, two for special highly desired practice areas, and another based upon a former background. The difference may only be slight, but the targeting has a special effect. It says: "I seriously want this special position."

A young graduate of a paralegal program wanted to do an extensive direct mail program after graduation. Latching on to the targeted resume concept, he came up with three resumes. He was very interested in insurance. He figured his youth and education would assist him in gaining a position that could begin a long career in a large industry. He also wanted to pursue the world of real estate, knowing it, too, covered a world of activity. He also wanted to have a resume that could serve his purpose of applying to "any and all" corporations that might have legally related positions that were not specifically termed "paralegal." The following resumes (Figures 5-8, 5-9, and 5-10) are targeted. Notice that the Skills section has been "massaged" to point toward the specific area of interest. His experience is basic and does not change from resume to resume. His education, you will notice, brings out different classes to suit each resume. He has employed the Objective and the Skills creatively so that the recipient sees phrases and buzz words that relate. This is sometimes the edge that an applicant needs to get called in for an interview. Since this young man was also using these resumes for direct mail programs, he was insuring that his investment in time and money would be most effective.

**Fig. 5-8**

                              Ronald Pagliacci
                           9995 E. Dartmouth Ave.
                            Houston, Texas 77077
                                 (Phone)

Objective:
   Paralegal with four-year business degree seeks entry-
   level position with a corporate, legal, administrative,
   or compliance department.

Education:
   Texas Paralegal Institute, August 1994. Paralegal
   Certificate. Curriculum covered commercial law, business
   organizations, legal research and terminology, civil
   litigation, legal investigations, and laws and issues
   related to liability and negligence.

   University of Northern Texas, B.A. Business
   Administration, December 1989. Finance emphasis.
   Coursework included business law, communication and
   public relations, accounting, finance, and management.

Relevant Skills:
   *   Extensive communication, problem-solving, and human
       relations skills.
   *   Skilled at analyzing and preparing legal and financial
       reports, forms, and memos.
   *   Able to research relevant laws and regulations related
       to business issues.
   *   Familiar with monitoring and tracking pending
       legislation.
   *   Adaptable to new situations, circumstances, and
       people.

Experience:
   Bank Temps Inc., Houston, Texas. Customer service and
   banking positions, June 1993 to present

   Western Temporaries, Ft. Worth, Texas. Data entry and
   customer service positions. March 1993–June 1993

   On Call Temp Services, Dallas, Texas. Data entry and
   banking positions. October 1992–March 1993

   Walgreen's Inc., Sugarland, Texas. Assistant Manager. May
   1992–September 1992

   Radio Shack, Bellaire, Texas. Salesman. August 1990–May
   1992

              REFERENCES AVAILABLE UPON REQUEST

Fig. 5-9

Ronald Pagliacci
9995 E. Dartmouth Ave.
Houston, Texas 77077
(Phone)

Objective:

Paralegal with four-year business degree seeks entry-level position in real estate or title work.

Education:

*Texas Paralegal Institute*, August 1994. Paralegal Certificate. Curriculum covered commercial law, real estate/title, business organizations, legal research and terminology, civil litigation, and legal investigations.

*University of Northern Texas*, B.A. Business Administration, December 1989. Finance emphasis. Coursework included business law, communication and public relations, accounting, finance, and management.

Relevant Skills:

* Familiar with real estate forms and procedures.
* Knowledgeable about researching public records and documents.
* Skilled at analyzing and preparing legal and financial forms and reports.
* Able to work independently and process large volumes of work quickly and accurately.
* Extensive communications and public relations skills.

Experience:

*Bank Temps Inc.*, Houston, Texas. Customer service and banking positions, June 1993 to present

*Western Temporaries*, Ft. Worth, Texas. Data entry and customer service positions. March 1993-June 1993

*On Call Temp Services*, Dallas, Texas. Data entry and banking positions. October 1992-March 1993

*Walgreen's Inc.*, Sugarland, Texas. Assistant Manager. May 1992-September 1992

*Radio Shack*, Bellaire, Texas. Salesman. August 1990-May 1992

REFERENCES AVAILABLE UPON REQUEST

**Fig. 5-10**

Ronald Pagliacci
9995 E. Dartmouth Ave.
Houston, Texas 77077
(Phone)

Objective:
Seeking an entry position in the insurance industry.

Education:
Texas Paralegal Institute, August 1994. Paralegal Certificate. Curriculum covered commercial law, real estate/title, business organizations, legal research and terminology, civil litigation, and legal investigations.

University of Northern Texas, B.A. Business Administration, December 1989. Finance emphasis. Coursework included business law, communication and public relations, accounting, finance, and management.

Relevant Skills:
* Familiar with basic insurance terms and policies.
* Acquainted with searching public and private records including police, medical, and legal.
* Knowledgeable about properly handling investigations.
* Able to research relevant laws, regulations, and cases related to insurance claims and issues.
* Able to work independently and meet deadlines.
* Adaptable to new situations, circumstances, and people.

Experience:
Bank Temps Inc., Houston, Texas. Customer service and banking positions, June 1993 to present.

Western Temporaries, Ft. Worth, Texas. Data entry and customer service positions. March 1993-June 1993.

On Call Temp Services, Dallas, Texas. Data entry and banking positions. October 1992-March 1993.

Walgreen's Inc., Sugarland, Texas. Assistant Manager. May 1992-September 1992.

Radio Shack, Bellaire, Texas. Salesman. August 1990-May 1992.

REFERENCES AVAILABLE UPON REQUEST

## Update Your Resume as Soon as You Get Work

If you secure temporary, part-time, or contract work in the legal field before you get a full-time permanent position, one of your first actions should be to update your resume. What many choose to do is bring the Education Section down to a level below Legal Experience. They lead with experience just obtained and then perhaps insert a paralegal internship underneath it. This is not the only way to handle it, but be certain you update your resume in some way that highlights your new paralegal-related work.

When you update your resume like this, you are showing a viability, ambition, and determination to establish yourself as a paralegal. **Some people tend to minimize temporary or part-time or contract experience because it is not their ultimate goal. Minimize it in your mind if you must, but take full advantage of it on your resume.** This advertisement is saying: "This person is flexible. This person wants to work. This person is getting valuable experience. Let's take a look."

## The Experienced Resume

The rule of thumb for an experienced paralegal is that work background is generally more important than education on a resume. Yes, there are exceptions to all these rules, but experienced paralegals are primarily advertising their professional status. For these individuals, the major shift in the resume is to bring the Education Section down and the Work Experience up to the top of the resume. Remember, *vagueness hurts.* When elaborating on the job description, the experienced paralegal needs to use specific sentences that are meaningful to attorneys. If you generalize, you might be perceived to be equivocating or embellishing the truth.

| | |
|---|---|
| Instead of: | "Assisted attorneys with discovery and trial prep." |
| Use: | "Handled witness interviews, deposition summaries, organization of trial exhibits, and indexing of all documents produced." |

The first phrase would cause a doubting person to question exactly what you did. Specific descriptions are always better than general ones. The potential employer may be looking for a certain kind of experience that you have handled. Some interviews are gained on small items that mean the difference between getting called and being overlooked.

Resume Rules of Thumb for the Experienced Paralegal:

1) Be sure everything is accurate and truthful. Legal communities are close-knit and smaller than you might realize. Misrepresentations can kill your chances for an interview.
2) Cover all the experience you had in a certain firm, not just the most recent or most important. You never know what is going to get you an interview, and thus, a job.
3) Use a Reference Sheet. Have three names on your resume that interested parties can call. It is important that you check with people first and be relatively sure that they will give you a glowing reference. If you have had a "difficult parting" with an individual at a firm, try to get a written letter of reference from someone who appreciated your contributions at that same firm.
4) Keep the same high standards you employed with your initial resume. A half-hearted, medium-quality resume does not make experience look better. Experience looks better on a beautifully done written advertisement.

## Summary

So, let us take a look at all that your resume must accomplish. It must first *stand out*, then *stand up* to scrutiny, then *stand with you* in your interview. A resume that looks great but which does not fit you or which misrepresents you is no good at all. In the interview, the whole package comes together; all elements must work harmoniously together in your bio or oral presentation. That is why your cover letters and resumes should hold you in a laudatory light. Your skills, as described in your resume, should all be drawn so that they are describing a potential working professional paralegal.

You use the resume and cover letter as your "script" to show a package that creates a compelling need to hire, as we stated in the chapter on interviewing. It must be a positive, well-considered, edited document from which you can persuasively interview. The resume is your anchor.

# CHAPTER 6

## Effective Written Presentations
### Putting Together Your Professional Paralegal Package

"I hate these things!" She tossed her cover letters across my desk and folded her arms in disgust. "Why can't we just send resumes?"

"This irritating duty, this necessary task, is what employers use to get a look at you, the individual." I picked up her samples and held them in my hand like playing cards. "They get you qualified, they get you disqualified. Because resumes tend to be at such a high minimum standard, because people spend scores of hours on and invest in resumes, the cover letter is seen as 'the real you.' Pay attention to it, care about it, double-check it and be creative with it and it will get you interviews you might not otherwise have gotten. Overlook it, dismiss it, and give little attention to it and it will lose you interviews you otherwise might have gotten." I leaned back and placed her letters in an array before me. "The more you appreciate these dynamics, the better you'll do. You might not ever *like* this task, but you can still take pride in putting together your professional paralegal package, beginning with a well-written cover letter."

The crowning achievement in your professional paralegal package is an effective written presentation—the cover letter. Writing a cover letter is outwardly simple, but the rub comes when paralegal applicants are *disqualified* because of this outwardly simple task. Getting disqualified in the beginning means you have no chance to exhibit the fine personal and professional qualities you have developed. **The purpose of a cover letter is to enliven interest in you as a person, causing close scrutiny of your resume.**

Cover letters are generally the last thing we do in creating the package. They are the quickest and simplest thing we do, but it is easy to forget that they are the *first* thing by which we are judged.

Your job search techniques and effective written presentations are inseparable. There is a kind of magic in this process, because there are so many variables and unknowns. You are judged by the total package. When they come together to create your desired professional image, they  really do have an "abracadabra" effect! **All written presentations should be designed to get you an interview.** Before you fire off a few hundred written letters to potential employers, let us step back and look at the job search process at this stage. Getting an offer in an interview happens because these basics of the "package" are in place.

## Considering the Basics of the Job Search

> *For want of a nail the shoe was lost,*
> *For want of a shoe the horse was lost,*
> *For want of a horse the commander was lost,*
> *For want of a commander, the battle was lost.*
> *For want of a battle, the kingdom was lost.*
> *And all for the want of a horseshoe nail!*
>
> —Olde English Proverb

A Little Mistake
Is as Big as a Big Mistake
If it takes you out of the Running.

Figure 6-1 displays the basics that every paralegal job seeker must utilize in beginning the job search process—things that are discussed in many employment workshops at schools and private seminars.

### Written parts of your professional package

First, there is the *cover letter.* You must have the ability to produce a high-quality cover letter within half a day—sometimes a full day is too long to wait. The letter should be typed; that is a basic minimum. Today's wordprocessors allow you to take the presentation one step further and let you create a cover letter that has the same physical qualities as your resume. If possible, use the same typeface as your resume, but definitely use the same bond paper.

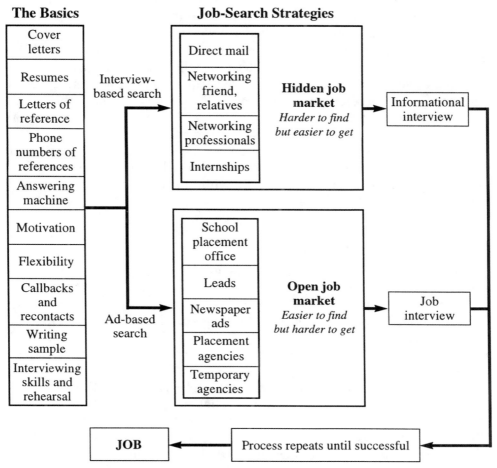

**Fig. 6-1** The Synergistic Job Search.

*Reference letters,* which you carry with you to an interview or slip into an envelope with your cover letter and resume, are very useful and can make a strong impression, though they do not make as powerful an impression as some think. Prospective employers assume that if someone writes a reference letter for you, it will seldom be anything other than complimentary. They need not be on bond; they can be photocopies.

*Oral references*, on the other hand, can be questioned and cross examined. List three references, making sure there is at least one attorney, preferably two. If you have past supervisors or similar associates, those are good. Avoid using the same individual for written and oral references. Some people make the mistake of putting family friends on this list. This is acceptable if he or she has worked with you in a professional capacity, but if the family friend is listed simply because he or she has known the family for a long time, the oral reference will not count for much. Internships offer excellent opportunities for acquiring both written letters of reference and oral references. Remember, the purpose of these references is to provide information to the would-be hiring entity about how you *work* as a professional.

The reference page should also be on the *same paper* as your cover letter and resume. Following this presentation will take your professional package out of the amateur class. But, without the other basics, you will not even be considered a contender.

## *Other basic elements of the professional package*

An *answering machine* (or someone who is always home) is an absolute must. Phone companies in many areas offer for nominal monthly fees a voice mailbox, but you may find an answering machine is the more economically reasonable choice in the long run. If a potential employer cannot leave a message for you on your phone, you are going to need more than your share of good fortune in order to become a professional paralegal.

*Motivation* and *flexibility* are important to consider at this time, because it is at this point that many realize what a commitment of physical resources, money, time, and effort it takes just to get to the starting line.  **The effective paralegal job search is like an election campaign. You must have enough resources in the beginning to run a "long haul."** If you want to attain and maintain your professional paralegal status, you must have the motivation and flexibility to sit in the quiet of your home and craft cover letter after cover letter, tailoring them to each contact. At times, this process will not seem to be efficient or economical. At times it could seem like a waste—until you make something happen. Then, when you get a few call backs, line up an interview or two, or deal with the possibility of a job offer, then your eyes light up and your energies flow to the front of the campaign and you realize—this can be done! I can do this! And then you will realize why the effective paralegal job search is seldom efficient, but it *is* indeed *effective*. And that effectiveness is judged in *interviews* and *job offers*.

When you conduct a *call-back campaign* to previous contacts, you can tell yourself, "If just *one* of these turns into an interview, that one interview could turn into a job." We will discuss call backs in more detail, but there is a balance to be struck with the phone and the paralegal job seeker. You must be assertive enough to call employers to whom you have sent letters, but smart enough to know when to stop calling. If you leave three messages but get no response within a period of a week or so, you can start to assume that you are not going to make progress on the phone and/or that you could be making a nuisance of yourself.

This is the basic attitudinal requirement you must incorporate into these job hunting basics. Repeat it over and over: **The goal of the effective paralegal job search is to get just *one* job**! After you become employed, don't retire your job hunting notebook; you still log professional contacts and insert "kudos" and letters of reference that will enhance your next job search.

The next stage of the basics involves having the necessary extras for the interview, such as *writing samples*, transcripts, and certificates. Briefs, motions, notices, legal memoranda, or pleadings could be utilized as writing samples. Make sure they are no longer than five pages. Many carry an interview portfolio that holds all of these.

There are two things not referred to in Figure 6-3 that are basic elements that may appear to be too obvious. Nevertheless they merit a passing reference: *clothing* and *transportation*. Wardrobe requirements can vary widely from firm to firm. Transportation to a job can be a problem for some, and a reliable car may be a requirement for some of the jobs. Also remember that some firms offer parking (especially in downtown settings) and others do not.

### The qualification/disqualification process

After considering the basics of your professional package, we are faced with a reality that must be acknowledged. It is the *qualification/disqualification process*.

> Janus, a Roman god, had two faces. Ever watchful, he was the guard of the temple. As you walk the road to your job, you must recognize the two faces of Janus, which are mirrored on the heads of the Janus Sentries: the face of qualification and disqualification. Imagine that you are on a mythical quest,

caught on a windswept cliff on a Hero's journey. At every pause you see a two-headed guard, watching your journey.

If the guard turns the smiling face at you, you can continue; if the sour expression leans toward you, you know you are in danger of being turned away. When you get the smile of approval, you are invited by the guard to pass on, and you merrily proceed, thankful that you have made it past another barrier.

The Janus Sentries exact the greatest toll early in the journey.

As you can see in Figure 6-2, disqualification process is the most ruthless at the beginning stages of the hire. At each stage the field is reduced, and the disqualification process continues to work, thinning the field. After the applicants have been basically qualified, then the urge to disqualify is more subtle. It takes on subjective and arbitrary characteristics in the interview stage. The message that is given to those in charge of reviewing the first group of applicants is basically, "Here are 25 cover letters and resumes; give me eight for the first interview."

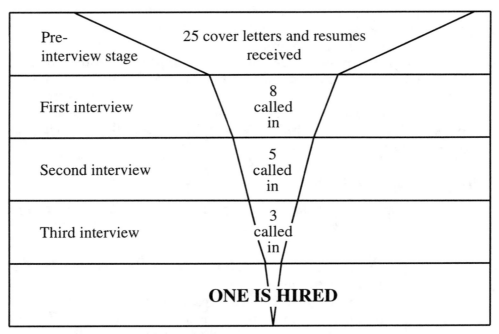

**Fig. 6-2** How the qualification/disqualification process works.

Figure 6-2 illustrates the importance of the cover letter in the first stages of the process, in which disqualification is more likely than qualification.

### A reason to network

A formal advertisement in a school, newspaper, or association will garner a large number of applicants. In a networking situation, the disqualification process is less in evidence. The mandate to scrutinize and reject you is not present, because you are not one of many applicants responding to an advertised lead. You may be the *only one* they are considering! This is another reason to choose networking over ad-based searches: Symbolically speaking, the back door is right next to the hiring door, while the front door is at the other end of a series of obstacles.

Responding to a formal advertisement is the most challenging job search method, and, because the odds are against you, it puts the written presentation and other job search basics in the forefront.

## Narrowing the Field—The Importance of an Effective Cover Letter

The person who is told to throw out 40 resumes will do so with a number of different standards in mind. The first elements we will deal with have to do with *basic standards*. These basic standards are fairly universal and must be met by all applicants. There are exceptions (people who get hired in spite of violating one or more of these standards), but they are exceptions that prove the rule.

In the hurry and tension of the job search process, the paralegal applicant must meet the basic requirements and craft a letter that creates an "above average" image. The most beautifully crafted letter, loaded with skills and meaningful experience—but *unsigned*—will most likely be rejected. This is the pressure you are under—write a good letter, cover all the basics, and don't forget to *sign* the cover letter.

A cover letter printed on a top-of-the-line laser printer on the most expensive bond that has misspelled a name in the firm is headed for the wastebasket. The best applicant who seems to fit the job better than any other can be rejected in the first disqualification stage, if there are typos on the cover letter. These standards are used because they reflect upon professionalism. They are also the easiest way to bring a group of 50 down to 10.

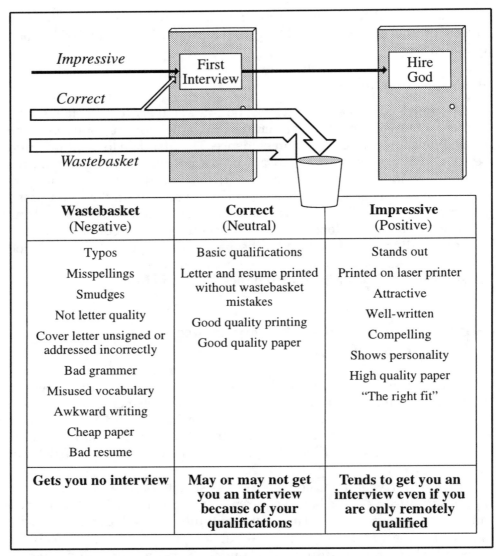

| Impressive | | |
| --- | --- | --- |
| Correct | First Interview | Hire God |
| Wastebasket | | |

| **Wastebasket** (Negative) | **Correct** (Neutral) | **Impressive** (Positive) |
| --- | --- | --- |
| Typos | Basic qualifications | Stands out |
| Misspellings | Letter and resume printed without wastebasket mistakes | Printed on laser printer |
| Smudges | | Attractive |
| Not letter quality | Good quality printing | Well-written |
| Cover letter unsigned or addressed incorrectly | Good quality paper | Compelling |
| Bad grammer | | Shows personality |
| Misused vocabulary | | High quality paper |
| Awkward writing | | "The right fit" |
| Cheap paper | | |
| Bad resume | | |
| **Gets you no interview** | **May or may not get you an interview because of your qualifications** | **Tends to get you an interview even if you are only remotely qualified** |

**Fig. 6-3** Reaching the office of the Hire God.

Notice the first column in Figure 6-3. The wastebasket column contains many (but not all) of the potential disqualifying mistakes that a fully qualified and completely professional paralegal applicant can make. *Note them.*

Your goal must be nothing less than *making sure you are not disqualified!* At times when individuals are frustrated, they call and ask me, "Why can't I get any interviews?" The first thing I tell them to do is to take a look at those cover letters. They could be too wordy, awkward, unfocused, impersonal, abrupt, or just riddled with grammatical and usage errors. In short, the cover letter could be the enemy; they did not even get to your resume. The disqualification process, especially at the early stages, can be dealt with by simply taking care, writing professionally, and going over and over your work.

### *The cover letter that is simply "correct"*

Many people simply write cover letters that are mistake-free, short, and "correct." This approach works because (1) you do not disqualify yourself with mistakes and (2) a short, terse cover letter points the reader to the resume, which is one of the purposes of the cover letter. **There is great virtue in not getting yourself disqualified by saying too much or being overly wordy.** But the merely "correct" letter often does not "jump out" at the reader and create a compelling reason to interview.

### *Why have a cover letter anyway?*

Many frustrated paralegals might ask this question. Cover letters serve some basic, but important, purposes:

1) They show the "person" behind the resume.
2) They test basic writing ability and level of professionalism.
3) They show how well you "fit" the particular job, firm, or situation that you are seeking.
4) They serve as a way of *comparing* applicants before interviews to help make interview decisions.

These four purposes show you why writing a letter that is merely "correct" and creates "*no* impression" can be a *liability* in the overall hiring process. A letter that is short and merely correct does not show much of the "person" (Purpose #1), but it does not hurt you, per se. It does reduce "rejectability factors" and thus helps you (Purpose #2). Since it is short and terse, it may not show how you "fit" the job, unless you are a "perfect fit" based upon your resume (Purpose #3). Since it shows so little of you, it probably does not give a full picture to assist in "comparing" you with competitors. And *competition* is the key word here.

### *Writing an impressive cover letter: how to beat the competition*

If this were not a competitive job market, a "safe" cover letter might do. But in a market in which many applicants are seeking positions (and thus more people are as qualified as you), impressive cover letters must have the following characteristics:

1) personality
2) the right fit
3) extra value offered

Ironically, one of the enemies of persuasive, enthusiastic, compelling cover letters is the personal computer. Because people *can* write standard cover letters and print them out as a "freshly created" letter, they *do*. They simply plug in different addresses and names and dates and print away. Before the PC, cover letters had to be typed individually each time. This put more stress on job applicants, but it also forced them to create individualized cover letters. You can get disqualified immediately if you send a cover letter printed out on a dot matrix printer on low-quality paper, with the feed guides torn from the side of the paper.

The quality, specificity, personality, and focus of cover letters would dramatically rise if people labored over cover letters just a few minutes longer each time one was written, to make sure that *that* particular written presentation was their best attempt at being compelling. **A compelling cover letter stands out because it reads as if it were written for the first time.** When a letter does not specifically address the job description, practice area, or some other unique quality, then it seems like a literal "cover letter"—something written to go on top of a resume simply because the rules say you have to write one. A successful cover letter will do the following:

1) addresses key issues in ad
2) shows enthusiasm.
3) written for specific firm or practice area
4) best quality paper and good typewriter or printer
5) well-constructed (reads easily and logically)
6) well-written (with correct grammar and vocabulary)
7) avoids all errors
8) calls for action (asks for interview or phone call)

The concept of *extra added value* is one that is heard in seminars concerning new management techniques and philosophies. Suffice it to say that the simple act of listing the contributions you can make, or qualities you bring to the job, or skills that constitute the package that is you, will make you stand out. The concept of added value is one that you must take with you to the interview and the resume, but it must begin with the cover letter. When you craft your cover letter, you are focusing on your best qualifying features. If all goes well, the recipient will meet you and discover the totality of you and your attributes. **Eighty percent of the hiring process takes place in the interview, so getting called for an interview is the primary goal of your resume and cover letter.** An impressive cover letter gets you noticed. If your cover letter has some personality and stands out from the crowd, it could be the edge you need to be interviewed. Paralegals who think the cover letter is just a "cherry that goes on top of the ice cream" are missing the dynamics of this very important part of the effective job search.

## Guidelines for writing an effective cover letter

A cover letter must be:

1) *One page in length.* No exceptions. A letter that is longer than one page means you are probably gushing, pleading, or explaining too much.
2) *Three paragraphs.* Make the following three points of emphasis:
   a) why you are writing and who you are
   b) skills, value, contribution you make to specific job or situation
   c) action step—ask them to take action or tell them the action you will be taking
3) *Written in the active voice.* Avoid the passive voice. Instead of "One point of emphasis is," write "I emphasize"; do not say "some of the skills that should be considered are," say, "Consider these skills." The passive voice tends to be a weak construction that people use when they are writing instead of when they are speaking. The direct active voice gives a feeling of vitality to your letter.
4) *Easy to read.* Do not use multisyllabic words when short, simple words will do. Overcomplicated letters that only attempt to impress and intellectualize defeat the purpose of the cover letter.

## The First Paragraph of the Cover Letter

The first paragraph, generally, should be no more than three to four sentences. State the purpose of your communication in the first sentence. The K.I.S.S. Rule (**Keep It Simple, Stupid**) applies here. This rule simply means, do not overthink this process. Get to the point, and when you are done, go on to the next; when you are done with all your points, quit.

Start with your most important points in the first paragraph: Who you are and *why* you are writing.

| | |
|---|---|
| THE "WHO": | A recent graduate of a paralegal program, a paralegal with experience in an internship, a paralegal with a certain kind of experience in certain practice areas. |
| THE "WHY": | If it is a networking letter, begin by referring to the name of the person who is the *key reference name*. That immediately identifies you with the reader. |
| | The *advertisement* to which you are responding. |
| | The *practice area* around which your interest/experience and their firm revolve. |
| | A *geographic area* to which you are moving. |
| | A *specialty kind of experience or educational background* which will make you stand out instantly. |

In the first two sentences you should have covered the basics:

I am a recent graduate of ABC Paralegal Institute and recently had a stimulating internship experience with a busy personal injury firm here in town. Since you practice in this area, I would like to speak with you about the potential of performing some contract work for you and your firm.

If you have a four-year degree, be sure to include that in your first paragraph.

In this opening, you are immediately addressing who you are and why you are contacting them. You have already qualified yourself in two ways and have offered a proposition. Since in this example we are not responding to a formal job advertisement, we lower the stakes with an offer of contract work. Attorneys are often much more willing to talk about occasional work than a full-time offer. Remember, your goal is to obtain an interview—to get seated in front of a decision maker. If you have not referred to full-time work in your cover letter, that does not mean therefore that you cannot talk about it in the interview. This is a secret to all approaches, whether they be written or oral. If in your opening statements you say something like. "I am available for part-time, temporary, contract, or full-time work," you will get more interest than if you ask for a full-time job alone. The reason is simple: The total number of full-time permanent openings is smaller than the total number of paralegal employment opportunities.

You are not committing yourself to every offer you get. The mere fact that you have broadened the area of discussion to include a wider array of work does not obligate you. *You must consider every offer, query, and interview and then decide which to accept.*

The "Law of Mutual Arising" is a Chinese concept that simply rephrases a Newtonian law of physics: "For every action, there is an equal and opposite reaction." People in sales are often instructed on how to lower resistance. They are told to be more "soft sell," so that people will be less defensive. The same thing applies in the cover letter. Ask for a job and the corresponding resistance will be, "Why, I don't have a job!" Ask for less (time for an interview or a part-time or temporary job) and the resistance to your request is lowered. So, one approach is to state that you are available for all types of work, instead of limiting your scope to a full-time job. This opens up more possibilities and reduces rejection. It is likely that a firm will have *some* kind of work, whether it be temporary, part-time, or contract. The other way to lower rejection through lowered stakes is to not ask for employment at all, but rather ask for *time.*

> I would appreciate an opportunity to sit down with you and discuss the role of paralegals in your practice area.

This can be phrased a number of ways, but the key point is that you are not asking for a *job*, you are seeking *time to talk* about the market place, the practice area you have designated, what it is like to work in a firm such as this, what particular problems or challenges the attorney faces which you might specifically be able to help with. This method is employed particularly in face-to-face networking, telemarketing, and just chatting with people socially; it *starts* with a paragraph in a cover letter.

In a fully engaged job search, you will be called on to write different kinds of cover letters. With most advertised leads, the direct approach is natural and logical. You are writing because of an ad. Easy. Most networking leads, however, were generated through your own effort and the efforts of your friends and associates, so the natural approach is to ask for an interview or a session in which you can freely discuss all upcoming potential openings. In *direct mail*, the theory is to open yourself up to as many possibilities as can be activated. You are working a "numbers game" and you invested dearly in a large mailing. Any conversation you can get, over the phone, or in person, has a monetary value to you. In the case of direct mail, you want to appear as accessible and flexible as possible. So, every time you write a cover letter, remember the first paragraph is to  focus on where you are coming from and what you are after. **Your opening paragraph should cover the WHO and the WHY and then close so that you can quickly get to your skills, value, and potential benefits.**

## The Second Paragraph

The second paragraph is the Skills/Value paragraph. This is your personal sales pitch. The core of your bio (oral presentation) in the interview lies in the structure of this paragraph. As you assemble your qualifications in the construction of this paragraph, you are also preparing the outline of your interview.

Remember, in these sentences you are trying to tie together your virtues (skills and values) in a logical and readable style.

> I gained paralegal experience as an intern where I assisted attorneys with trial preparation, deposition summarizing, and document organization. I also used well-developed computer skills in drafting motions and preparing indexes. Since I have three years of office experience in a busy medical clinic, I combine a strong knowledge of medical terminology with a real sensitivity to client contact issues.

The elements covered in this sample second paragraph are:

1) Reiterated elements from first paragraph with an expansion of *specific skills and experiences gained.* As was previously mentioned, if you have a *four-year degree* be sure to introduce that fact in your *first paragraph.* Never neglect to include all of your paralegal training in this paragraph.
2) *Technical/computer skills* need to be in almost all cover letters. Elaborate on the systems you know. Mention the technical skills you have developed! Your competition does.
3) Introduce pertinent skills and experience from your *past background* such as work habits, or similarity of situation, that could be particularly meaningful to a practice area. *Transferability of skills* is the goal of each "Transitional Person." Since this profession is filled with "Transitionals," this is a goal you should strive for. The Skill Assessment Exercise in Chapter 5 is the forge from which your material will emerge. Don't fail to extract transferable skills from your background in a meaningful and credible way.

## PARALEGAL BUZZ WORDS

### ORGANIZATIONAL SKILLS:

stay calm under pressure . . . enjoy handling big projects . . . handle high interruptive environment . . . know how to stay on top of a large case load . . . am able to put out a great deal of work

### WRITING/RESEARCH SKILLS:

researched, drafted, and prepared reports or motions or pleadings, etc. . . . . drafted correspondence . . . prepared lists, reports, tables, statistics . . . know how to research . . .

### OFFICE SKILLS:

wordprocessing skills . . . able to type . . . willing to do own support work . . .

### SCHEDULING/DETAIL SKILLS:

detail orientation . . . accounted for . . . accounting . . . systems analysis . . . numbers . . . calculations . . . handling the small stuff while still keeping the big picture

### FLEXIBILITY:

willing to roll up sleeves and do the grunt work, but able to handle clients . . . stay late to get job out the door . . .

### INTERPERSONAL SKILLS:

skilled at dealing with people under stress . . . warm personality . . . able to keep poise and confidence and yet am a team player . . . not egotistical . . . not temperamental . . . can subordinate personal to the larger good . . . can adapt to various personalities . . . know how to deal with demanding people

### PROBLEM-SOLVING SKILLS:

resourceful . . . handled investigations . . . follow projects through to completion . . . can deal with theory and principle yet still armed with lots of practical skills that make me invaluable . . . know where to get answers, have professional skills to apply to problem-solving situations, believe in being able to get things done, and if I cannot, I ask the right questions and do the homework

### Paralegal "Buzz" Words

Figure 6-A designates and describes the kind of work paralegals do and the prevailing atmosphere in many firms. It is a stream of descriptive statements that should assist you in emphasizing the skills and experience that are meaningful to the person making hiring decisions. The main point is to emphasize *skills* more than *titles*. Do not use all of these phrases in a cover letter (for example, some would be more fitting in an interview), but reading these buzz words helps you define those past skills and experiences which would transfer most readily to the legal/paralegal market. Focusing on these skills will help you separate those experiences that were important to your last job from the skills that are meaningful and impressive to the person who might hire you for your *next* job.

## Two ditches to avoid

The cover letter is in many cases your first contact with a potential employer. It is crucial that you avoid typical pitfalls, and walk the correct and middle path in the job search process. This path speaks confidently about your virtues and skills, but does not boast, stretch credibility, sound excessive, or go to extremes. The "Superior Ditch" is the ditch into which many fall. Some think bravado will disguise itself as confidence, and that enthusiasm will "out-shout" a lack of qualifications. Overconfidence, boastfulness, and a "know-it-all" attitude get applicants rejected more than any other negative qualities.

The "Inferior Ditch" also causes rejection, because law firms are not in the business of acquiring muted, self-effacing, meek, and monosyllabic professional assistance. People who transmit the message that "they are not worthy" and that they are dwarfed by their surroundings get rejected at nearly the same rate as those who act too superior. Law firms and other legal settings need support personnel who can honestly present their skills and talents in a positive and declarative manner. Hiring managers want strong people who can handle the stress of professional life, not people who appear to wither under the pressure of stress and tense interpersonal dynamics.

While this problem is most visible in the interview, it actually begins in the written presentation phase of the job search process.

The Skills/Value paragraph of your cover letter is the first tangible experience you have with the delicate balance of inferiority vs. superiority. In the cover letter you are challenged to present yourself in a credible and positive manner, not only as a believable "fit" but also a "perfect fit." As you craft your second paragraph, attempt to keep this dynamic in balance.

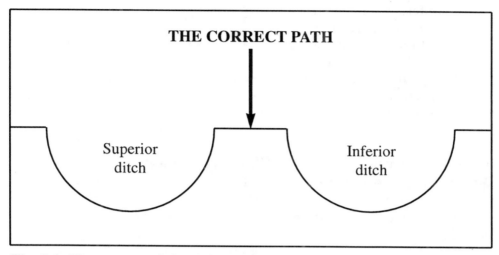

**Fig. 6-4** The correct path for oral and written presentations.

## The Third Paragraph—Do Not "Fade to Black"

In movies and TV, the signal that a scene is about to end is the "fade to black"—the picture gradually darkens until the screen is completely black. The worst thing you can do in your third paragraph is fade to black. Avoid paragraphs like the following:

> Thank you very much for taking the time out of your very busy schedule to peruse my resume. Although I have little experience, I still think that someone with my particular background could be a good paralegal. Thanks again for taking the time to read this.

This paragraph is weak and apologetic. *It cries out for an action step.* Compare it to this:

> I am looking forward to discussing your practice with you, and I will be calling you in ten days to see if we can arrange an interview.

If you are arriving in town, note that in your last paragraph. Ask them to call you—it's the logical consequence of your letter. If you fail to call for some kind of action, your letter will sound weak and pleading or nondirected and unenthusiastic. A fade to black third paragraph is downbeat and leaves a wrong impression. Use the following steps to help you write your action paragraph:

a) reiterate your interest
b) talk about availability
c) tell them to call you or
d) tell them you will call
e) explain special circumstances
f) be professional
g) don't beg

## Common Pitfalls to Avoid When Writing Your Cover Letter

The following examples are not exaggerations. Most are taken from actual letters.

1) **Awkward sentences and incorrect punctuation.** "I have experience in drafting motions, motions for summary judgment and default judgment being some of them, though not all; with pleadings being occasional and sporadic."

2) **Overly complex sentences.** "Though I have a strong professional background with management and administration, I am still able to take orders and facilitate projects in a teamwork setting; taking into account that my best work is really done when I am unsupervised and in a self-directed situation."

3) **Excessive explaining.** "I used to work on WordStar and the initial WordPerfect system and feel that my typing skills, though adequate now, could be rapidly improved. Since you have asked for experience on Macintosh, I think that I could easily train into that in a matter of days."

4) **Too personal.** "Through a series of personal changes that took place in my life in the last two years, I find myself in your city and very anxious to reestablish myself so that I can get on solid ground and . . . "

5) **Too desperate.** "I am anxious to speak with you about this opportunity. The combination of my enthusiasm, curiosity, and ambition will make me a great employee. If I can only be given the chance to speak with you . . . "

6) **Too formal.** "Please be informed that I am submitting my application for employment in the form of this letter and its accompanying resume. Note my educational background and an attached letter of reference for your perusal and consideration."

7) **Flattering assumptions.** "A firm with your commitment to the highest of ethical and professional standards with a strong reputation in the community and a dynamic and progressive point of view would be . . ."

8) **Too short.** "Enclosed is my resume for your advertised job opening. Please call me if we can arrange an interview."

9) **Sounding overqualified.** "With my 20 years of administration and management experience, I am certain that I possess all the needed skills to accomplish whatever task that might arise in the office."

10) **Using self-limiting statements.** "Though I have no legal experience, I feel I could . . . "

11) **Not employing "buzz words"**

12) **Not signing your letters**

13) **Not using language appropriate to specific practice areas**

14) **Misspelling**

15) **Date, margins, spacing errors**

## Cover Letters: Tiny Works of Art

Good cover letters are made up of many elements. First, they get to the point. You will notice from many of the negative examples just cited that they have a shapeless quality. They try to include too much, but say little. Good letters are easy for an intelligent, interested person to read. They do not belabor points, but breeze along quickly. They are straightforward, avoiding timidity or brashness. They attempt to be descriptive to a certain degree, using adjectives and adverbs when appropriate. *They sound like a real person:* They use enthusiasm and positiveness, which they know are infectious. They envision a relationship of *mutual benefit,* derived from the *value* that the applicant offers, and from the *opportunity* within the firm. They do not sound ostentatious or haughty; they use appropriate vocabulary and correct grammar.

All of these elements together make a good cover letter. The challenge is not to write an "unforgettable piece of literature," but to spend enough time crafting these "tiny works of art" so that they beautifully reflect you, the professional paralegal, and your particular individual worth!

## The Direct Mail Cover Letter

Creating a written presentation for a direct mail campaign is a particular challenge. You must write a letter that can go to a group of 50, 100, or 200 attorneys in a given city, or practice area or combination of geography/practice area. The goal then is to write a presentation that will have broad appeal and present a basically qualified and professional image.

Please refer to Figure 6-5. This "variable document," which was created by a paralegal applicant, is a good example of a letter designed to go to a metropolitan area. All practice areas are targeted. She is attempting to get an interview with anyone who might have an opening.

A good direct mail cover letter neatly and crisply sums you up and supplies a snapshot of a qualified applicant. Without an advertisement or other connecting element to refer to, the letter should get to the point: Talk about your qualifications, ask for an interview, tell them you will call them, and close. It helps you focus on your basic skills and qualifications, and forces you to formally delineate them. A well-done, direct mail, written presentation can be the backbone of all of your other letters and the core of the "bio" that you create for your interviews.

Also, please observe Figure 6-6, which is a direct mail cover letter written to a specific corporation or firm. In this kind of letter, the focus is on the company. *The company is mentioned in the letter.* This has much more focus and will be read with more interest by the employer. This kind of treatment can also be done with the use of a variable document. The name of the firm is in the body of the letter, because a command has been set up to insert it at that point.

**Fig. 6-5**

1~
2~
3~
4~

ATTN:     5~

Dear 5~:


I have recently completed the ABA-approved General
Practice program at ABC Paralegal Institute and am
interested in working in the Chicago area. I would be
interested in talking with you about how I could
assist you in your practice.

As noted on my enclosed resume, I graduated from the
University Center at Tulsa with a degree in business
management last May. In addition to my education, my
background includes an internship with Mr. Dick Tracy,
Esq. of Investigative Reporting Services in Tulsa. At
this internship, I gained experience not only in the
legal profession but in investigative practices as
well. I also have training and experience in
WordPerfect 5.1 and Lotus and am proficient in their
uses.

I would like to discuss your practice with you and
explore ways in which I could make a contribution to
your firm. I will call your office within the next
week to set up an appointment.

Thank you for your interest and consideration, and I
look forward to meeting you.

Sincerely yours,

## Practice, Practice, Practice

Your skills for writing effective cover letters will improve with practice. In preparation for your job hunt, you may want to write a few sample cover letters before you are under the gun to respond to competitive job opportunity. Try writing the following:

- Write your own general direct mail cover letter. Include your background, education, skills. Conclude with a positive action step.
- Write a cover letter based upon a third party networking connection, in which you are asking for time to discuss paralegal work in a specific practice area, and any additional names of individuals who might be in need of paralegals in this practice area.
- Write a cover letter to an advertised lead from your school's placement board or the local newspaper.

## Sample Cover Letters

Compare Figures 6-7, 6-8, and 6-9 against each other. Decide which letter you like the best and for what reasons. These letters were all written to the same employer, in response to the following newspaper ad:

Statutorily created company which acts as a kind of Receiver for Insolvent Insurance companies seeks trained paralegals to deal with policyholders and policy issues. Insurance background helpful. Must be able to deal with people under stress and explain insolvency situation and policyholder options.

*Note:* All three of these people were interviewed and hired from a large group of applicants.

Fig. 6-6

1883 Silver Road
Moline, IL 61266
December 6, 1994


Legal Department
Deere & Company
John Deere Road
Moline, IL 61265-8098

Dear Sir or Madam:

I am very interested in a Paralegal position with Deere & Company. Growing up in Iowa has made me very familiar with your company.

I have a Paralegal Certificate from ABC Paralegal Institute, which is ABA approved. In addition, I have practical paralegal experience that has provided on-the-job knowledge of court rules, legal procedures, terminology, and legal research and writing. I have obtained this practical experience from my internship with the Illinois Attorney General's Office in the Antitrust and Consumer Protection Sections. I am continuing to perform paralegal duties with the Illinois Attorney General's Office.

I am proficient with WestLaw, WordPerfect, and Quattro Pro software. Employers and references state that I possess good oral and written communication skills, a good work ethic and professionalism, and the ability to work well under pressure.

I am looking forward to discussing my qualifications with you. I hope to hear from you soon.

Sincerely,


Aaron Schmidt

Fig. 6-7

1777 El Dorado Dr.
New City, IL 34567
December 6, 1994

Hiring Manager
Holding Company, Inc.
3232 Superior Road
New City, IL 34566

Dear Sir or Madam:

I have recently graduated number one with a 4.0 G.P.A. in a class of fifty-nine at the New City Paralegal Institute. I was given your name by the Career Development Counselor about a temporary position with your firm. I feel that an excellent way to begin a paralegal career is through temporary work and would be most interested in interviewing with you for this position.

In addition to my education, my background includes over three hundred hours of internship experience dealing with Plaintiff's personal injury claims. Because of my experience in dealing with insurance companies, I feel I would be an excellent candidate for this position.

I am presently on a temporary assignment which ends this Friday, but I would be able to interview with you at your convenience and will be available for work starting Saturday. I am very much looking forward to meeting you and can be reached at the numbers on my resume.

Sincerely,

Jerry Frank

**Fig. 6-8**

32 Main Street
New City, IL 34567
December 6, 1994

Hiring Manager
Holding Company, Inc.
3232 Superior Road
New City, IL 34566

Dear Sir or Madam:

Ellen O'Hara has informed me that you have a temporary position open for a paralegal with an insurance background. The position sounds very interesting to me. I have a paralegal certificate from New City Paralegal Institute, and many years of experience in the insurance industry.

I am very enthusiastic, detail-oriented, a good listener who can follow instructions, and a quick learner. I feel that my experience and qualities would make me an excellent candidate for your position, and I would sincerely like to meet with you personally to discuss it. I am available for work immediately.

Thank you for your time, and I hope to hear from you soon.

Sincerely,

Danielle Kenney

Fig. 6-9

199 Center Street
New City, IL 34567
December 6, 1994

Hiring Manager
Holding Company, Inc.
3232 Superior Road
New City, IL 34566

Dear Sir or Madam:

Ellen O'Hara has informed me of the opening for a Paralegal to work on an insurance company insolvency. I would very much like to be considered for this position.

As detailed within my enclosed resume, I have a strong and varied background in business management. During my many years of past management experience, I was directly involved in various forms and degrees of customer and client contact. By virtue of this experience, I have perfected my customer service skills by utilizing effective communication and listening techniques. As a result, I am very sensitive to the customer's needs.

I feel very strongly that my previous work experience, along with my legal education and strong work ethic will allow me to meet your objectives. Thank you for reviewing my resume; I look forward to hearing from you soon.

Sincerely,

Denise Allen

# CHAPTER 7

## *The Synergistic Job Search*
### *Becoming a Member of the "Hire" Order*

The leader of the seminar for new graduates began with a startling statement. "Getting over the entry-level hump is probably the most challenging thing a job seeker can do. No matter what field, the entry status is the most difficult to face; from theater to carpentry, from dentistry to the arts, the beginner must bring energy, perseverance, creativity, and hard work together to get through that phase."

A man in the back row raised his hand. "Isn't it just luck and knowing the right person?"

That question stopped the speaker for a moment. Then she continued, "Sometimes people get lucky. Sometimes people have a key connection. But the way to approach this challenge is to say, 'I will take advantage of good fortune with hard work. I will take advantage of connections *and* make my own connections. I will find out what works and then do all those things at once.'"

## The Value of the Synergistic Job Search

What is *The Synergistic Job Search?* The word *synergism* comes from the worlds of chemistry, biology, and physics. When things work synergistically, they work together to create an effect that could not exist if the two or more agents were acting alone and separately. Certain drugs can work synergistically. Certain nutrients and vitamins, when taken in a prescribed way can have a new and synergistic benefit.

*Synergism*—Working together. The action of two or more substances, organs or organisms to achieve an effect of which each is individually incapable. The "sum of the parts is greater than the whole."

**The *synergistic job search* is a way of working so that you get the maximum benefit out of everything you do.** Applicants who conduct a synergistic job search get hired more frequently than those who conduct a sporadic job search. The synergistic job search is nothing more than performing all recommended steps in their order, and mounting an *effort* that could be said to be "completely occupying." It involves doing all the follow-up in each phase of activity at the appropriate time so that your job search takes on a life of its own. Connections are generated through direct mail. Follow-up letters are sent to "nice rejection letters." Long-lost relatives become professional networking sources. You create a web of activity, a maximum effort, that helps you climb the entry-level hump and get around that phase in your career. Once you have entry experience, you are in new territory. You can successfully compete in the professional world to which you aspire. In this chapter we compare two contrasting efforts: the synergistic job search and the sporadic disconnected job search.

---

The **Synergistic Job Search** is a determined, persistent, professional effort waged simultaneously on all fronts, highlighted by direct mail, networking, the pursuit of advertised leads, continuing written follow-up, and high levels of personal contact, in order to benefit from the maximizing of *all* contacts. The result is a circuitry of contacts that is powered not only by individual effort but by the energy of the network created.

---

## The Sporadic Disconnected Job Search

To better understand the synergistic job search, we will contrast it with its opposite: the sporadic disconnected job search, as conducted by Bill Doolittle.

First, a word about taking time off after graduation. After completing a difficult paralegal program many paralegal candidates feel that they need to take some time off to recuperate. Bill certainly feels that way: He plans to rest up before going on to make an all-out effort. The sad fact for many is that they rest up for a week or two (or a month), and then begin a sporadic disconnected job search. This is what Bill does. His sporadic job search looks like this on a calendar:

Sunday: Check out the newspaper. Look under "Paralegal" and "Legal Assistant."

Monday: Write up cover letters and send resumes to two advertised openings.

Tuesday: Call local paralegal program and ask for new job leads.

Wednesday: Write cover letter and resume to new school-generated lead.

Thursday: Since Bill's been working all week, he takes off Thursday and Friday.

Bill Doolittle does not join local paralegal associations. He does not read the classified sections thoroughly to discover jobs that may be described in various ways "legal" or "paralegal." He neglects to even respond to advertised leads the next week. Because he has built up so little momentum, he finds it very easy to let inertia slow him down even more. Bill does not network with friends, relatives, and loved ones for potential contacts. He does not use direct mail and so does not generate any new contacts. When he does get an interview, he forgets to send a thank you note.

After a month of this kind of sporadic and furtive activity, Bill Doolittle begins to feel tired and discouraged, and he blames the marketplace for the lack of job offers. He eventually gets another interview, but by this time he has sunk into a quagmire of blame and irritation. The interview does not go well, because the "legal administrator had an attitude." A relative comes up with the names of several attorneys, but letters are never written. Like so many sporadic and disconnected searches, opportunities died on the vine, others are nipped in the bud, and connections do not get watered with the kind of follow-up that causes professional lives to thrive.

After a bout with depression and more inactivity, Bill starts to feel like his "brain is leaking" all the paralegal information he learned in the last few months. He starts to tell himself he was not right for the profession anyway. He never started on the right foot or put enough energy into the search. He did not take advantage of the web of connections, names, and opportunities that would have been generated by an energetic array of written and oral communications, since he never believed in a networking creed and thus never acted on that belief. Bill ends up fulfilling his own prophecies about his inability to fit into the profession.

## The Tools at Our Disposal

Before describing the process of the synergistic job search, let us look into the box of tools that we will use to become a member of the "hire" order. First, there are the oral presentations:

1) *Interviews.*   All kinds of interviews, styles, and situations will present themselves to you. The key is to be ready with a professional, warm, and upbeat personal presentation. (See Chapter 4.)

2) *Telemarketing.*   Follow-up phone calls based upon mailings made. "Cold calls" for contact names and other needed information such as practice areas and correct addresses and spellings of names. Telephone interviews conducted in place of a first interview.

3) *Social interactions.*   Parties, meetings, churches, restaurants, bars, cafes, gas stations, etc. You must always keep professionalism and the job search in mind as you flow through your life. The synergistic interconnectedness of the social with the professional is something that many people often overlook. They think of the social world and the work world as two different highways, connecting different houses and towns. **Keep in mind, workers socialize and socializers work. They are all the same people.** Lunches, breakfasts, and dates at cafes can all be useful ways of presenting yourself, cementing old relationships, having informational interviews, and just chatting with successful paralegals. And when you join organizations and associations, be prepared to speak up and meet people. Do not join a professional association and then become a "wallflower."

4) *Public speaking.*   You may be called upon to lead meetings or to introduce speakers or to be a speaker in an evening meeting or luncheon. Public speaking is not demanded frequently, but if you are effective, you can make a strong impression. The most common situation paralegals confront is simply speaking up in meetings at work.

Then there are the written presentations:

1) *Cover letters.* The basic cover letter announcing your availability and your skills and qualifications should be prepared in at least an outline form. From this skeleton, you customize elements of your cover letters.

2) *Follow-up letters.* In a Synergistic Job Search, all of your efforts are connected by oral and written follow-up. A chance meeting at a bar on a Friday night in which you get a business card and an invitation to "call me and we can talk about a future paralegal opening" should be officialized with a follow-up letter that next week.

3) *Direct mail letters.* Based upon the idea that a number of letters can "uncover" an unadvertised opening, these letters should be crafted for:
   a) any potential paralegal opening (part time, temp, contract, permanent)
   b) targeted openings (practice specific)
   c) geographic-specific openings
   d) combination ("I am writing to all personal injury firms in Smithville.")

4) *Networking letters.* These letters also officialize and confirm professional contacts. It is with the networking letter that you can truly generate and continually renew your network. These are a part of your professional development as you proceed beyond your entry employment. A networking letter opens with the connection. For example: "I enjoyed discussing your practice with you at The Elegant Saloon last Friday and would like to take you up on your offer . . . "; "My Uncle, James Shapiro said that you were a close friend and professional associate . . . "; "Municipal Judge Smith told me that your busy practice might need some legal support help. . . ."

5) *Thank you notes.* These can be a standard letter. After an interview, it makes a strong impression on the employer to see who will send a thank you note. This is often a hidden qualifier that makes you stand out. After all, you know the next round of interviews will be smaller than the previous round—you want to be a part of the new group.

6) *Letter accepting job.* This is a great way to confirm and officialize a decision. If you are starting a job in two weeks, you should write

a letter that says you have accepted an offer. This is an extremely professional touch that many overlook.

7) *Reconsideration letter.*   If you have had an excellent round of interviews and developed a strong feeling for the firm and then you are not chosen, write a letter and ask them to reconsider, or keep you in mind, if things do not work out.

### *Your personal network: get people to think about you even when you aren't thinking about you*

One night, when you can steal two hours, sit down with a pen and paper and start writing. Do not stop too soon. Sit there and document all of your friends and relatives. These are the people who really care about you. Then document your acquaintances. These are people who may not care about you as a loved one, but people who can nevertheless help you out because you are known to them. After you have finished your list, meet with these people. Tell them you are in a quest to find employment as a paralegal and want to elicit their help. The human desire to help is very strong; take advantage of it. Get people to think about you and your situation. Tell them you need names. Ask them to be on the lookout for attorneys or situations in law firms or legal settings. Remember, most all companies and corporations have attorneys working for them or in them. Sit down with your family and ask them to think of everyone they know who would not mind giving you some help. Tap in to the natural interconnectedness of your existing life, and let that work for you.

## A Synergistic Job Search Week

> Objects in Motion Tend to Stay in Motion
> Objects at Rest Tend to Stay at Rest
> Synergistic Job Seekers Tend to Stay in Motion
> Sporadic Job Seekers Tend to Stay at Rest

Employ the tools described above in a continuous flow of productive activity that keeps you in motion. The job search is challenging all by itself, but if you must overcome inertia all the time it can be agony. The key to using these tools is to *use* them at every turn. One way to stay in motion is to be active—initiate, follow up, and conduct continuous record-keeping. A synergistic job search week might look something like this:

Sunday:        Read entire newspaper. Check business section out
               for articles concerning lawsuits, regulatory situa-
               tions, mergers, bankruptcies, hirings, firings, profits,
               and losses. Go through the classified ads and read
               columns that pertain to legal and paralegal, but also
               areas such as insurance, administrative, and mana-
               gerial.

               Clip out all related and relevant articles and ads
               and place them in your Journal of Professional
               Contacts (your job hunting notebook with a new
               name—this is discussed and illustrated at the end
               of this chapter).

               After you are employed, keep this notebook and
               add writing samples from your work, letters that
               commend your efforts, professional association
               memberships, certificates from seminars and work-
               shops, and any other written material that will
               substantiate, validate, and perpetuate your profes-
               sional viability.

               Begin to prepare cover letters for mailing on
               Monday. Plan your week. You have made a direct
               mail campaign of sending out 25 letters a week
               with follow-up phone calls. This week you are
               going to call on the 25 from last week. This week
               you are sending out 25 new letters.

Monday:        Make mailing of 25 new letters to targeted list.
               Make mailings to advertised leads. Call on any ads
               that have given a phone number and that have
               indicated that you can call first thing Monday
               morning. *Note:* Unless you have been given a phone
               number in an ad, do *not* make phone calls on
               Monday morning. This is the least pleasant part of
               the week and you will meet with the strongest
               resistance at this time. Follow-up phone calls,
               networking phone calls, and cold calls will get the
               best reception between the hours of 10:00 A.M. to
               4:00 P.M. Tuesday through Thursday. For Monday
               mornings and Friday afternoons, the job searcher
               should plan other fruitful activities. Monday after-
               noon and Friday mornings are borderline. Remem-

ber, you want to reach your target when they are most likely to receive your call positively.

Tuesday: Write letter of application to local paralegal association or become an associate member of the local bar association. Call one of your fellow graduates to meet for a cup of coffee to help each other out in the job search. Make three follow-up phone calls on Tuesday morning concerning the 25 previously sent letters. You have one good connection from a mailing you made two weeks before. The attorney said you could come by and talk about some potential part-time work. You schedule this appointment with an eye toward getting five names from this attorney who could constitute a group for a networked mailing. You also might want to do some part-time work. Tuesday afternoon you make three more follow-up phone calls to the previous week's mailing.

Wednesday: You have the interview with the attorney who had some part-time work. She wants some short-term help with a trial coming in a month. You agree to help her. She gives five names and allows you to use her name in the cover letter. You go home and make that mailing of five, using her name in the first paragraph of your letter. You make six follow-up phone calls on Wednesday afternoon. No one wants to talk to you today. You are tired and excited. You go out with a recently employed paralegal friend who boosts you up and cheers you on. You get some exercise to relieve stress.

Thursday: In the morning you make your follow-up phone calls for last week's mailing. One person tells you to call in a month. Another person wants to speak with you about a secretary-paralegal position. Although you are not sure it sounds appealing, you schedule an interview for the experience. You get a call from one of the letters you sent on Monday from Sunday's paper, and schedule the interview for next week on your calendar. At your Thursday night bar meeting you volunteer to answer the phone and help out attorneys in their pro bono program. You log each attorney's name for future reference.

Friday: You sit down with your calendar and Journal of Professional Contacts and fill in the necessary information concerning your week's activities. You collect all the phone numbers you will be calling next week. You fill out your interview analysis sheets, lead sheets, and networking log concerning this week's activities. A youth group friend from church calls you and tells you that he has just met an attorney who might need some help. You thank him and quickly write a networking letter that will be on their desk on Monday so you can call them on Tuesday. You write a thank you note to the two people you have seen this week. You get a job rejection phone call late Friday afternoon. You quickly sit down and craft a letter of thanks and reconsideration and ask them to call you "if things do not work out with the one you have chosen." You are very disappointed, but at 4:30 on Friday afternoon, one of the firms who you wrote to four weeks ago calls you out of the blue and asks if you are still available. You try to sound calm and composed and agree to meet them next week. It seems one of their paralegals has suddenly given notice and will be gone in two weeks. Your letter just happened to be the most recent arrival on the legal administrator's desk.

Saturday: You sit yourself down on Saturday morning and tell yourself that you are not going to suspend all job search activity just because you are excited. You will continue your 25 letter direct mail campaign. You will keep your appointments and your record-keeping and all of your synergistic job hunting until you accept an offer and not before.

The whole point of this process is to carry every connection out to its last potential. If you speak with someone, have you written to them? If you speak with anyone in a position of influence, get some names from them. Many people get names from unsuccessful job interviewing situations. The dialogue might go like this:

*Interviewer:*    "We are truly sorry you were not chosen, but we think you have excellent qualifications."

*You:*    "Well, thank you, can you think of anyone else who might be interested in someone with my capabilities?"

## The Nice Rejection Letter—The Synergistic Job Search Response

If you get a rejection letter that says they might be busy in a few months or indicates that at sometime in the future they could be interested in you, you are looking a potential job in the eye, but not if *your* eyes are closed. Rejection letters tend to be pleasant, but they also tend to have very standard language that sounds formal. If the letter goes out of its way to offer some hope, or mentions a date in the future at which time they might be hiring, do not ignore it. The Sporadic Job Searcher just throws the letter away. But be creative. As many have been in the past, you can turn that "Nice Rejection Letter" into a positive! First, you log a recontact on your calendar. Then you act on a response when the date comes up:

Dear Mr. Attorney:

When I wrote to you in May, you indicated that your firm might be looking for a paralegal around the middle of August. I am still interested in your firm and would enjoy meeting with you to discuss your firm's workload as we approach the end of the year. . . .

In attempting to create a picture of success, this text explores the different avenues that successful paralegals use to travel the path to employment. Compared with the Sporadic Disconnected Job Search, the picture is more difficult to draw because of avenues not traveled at all, not traveled well, or not traveled at the right time. Suffice it to say that lack of success can be described in these ways:

1) *Omissions.*   The outright *omission* of certain avenues of activity, such as solely utilizing newspaper ads, not calling the school's placement departments, not using direct mail as a tool, not joining professional associations.

2) *Not traveling the avenues well!*   Some people are simply lax and slipshod in preparing their professional package. They do it, but the quality is off. They make too many basic errors. *Note:* These people can be helped if they will get job search assistance counseling from their Placement Department.

3) *Avenues not traveled at the right time.*   In so many aspects of life, timing is everything. It is especially true of the job search. Those who are sporadic tend to time it all poorly. They are a "day late and a dollar short." Many fail at being there early in the quest for advertised openings. Some jobs are filled in 48 to 72 hours. Timing is also essential in follow-up. If you wait too long, you are forgotten. If you harass the next day, you are an annoyance. If you try a direct mail campaign and then do not do follow-up until weeks later, you have lost the value of the direct mail.

   *Warning:* Haste does make waste. A Chinese philosopher said, "Hasten slowly." When you are in the job search, be on time, but do not lose control of the process, such as by making mistakes on cover letters or being overanxious in interviews. Tripping over yourself as you hurry to be correct, on time, just right, can make you err in many ways. Don't hurry quickly; instead, hasten slowly.

## The Synergistic Job Search—The Hiring Zone

The synergistic job searcher is always in the *hiring zone.* The sporadic disconnected job searcher weaves in and out of the hiring zone, with job search efforts that are poorly timed, intermittent, or flawed.

### Professional associations

Participating in local paralegal organizations helps you develop professionally with special seminars and expertise garnered from others and lets you access jobs through Job Banks and personal networking. It also enhances your resume by demonstrating that you care about the progress and development of your profession. In addition, you can develop leadership characteristics, practice public speaking, and sharpen your interpersonal skills. A side benefit is the "camaraderie," that is, the sense that you can share your gripes and your exaltations with people who are going through similar circumstances.

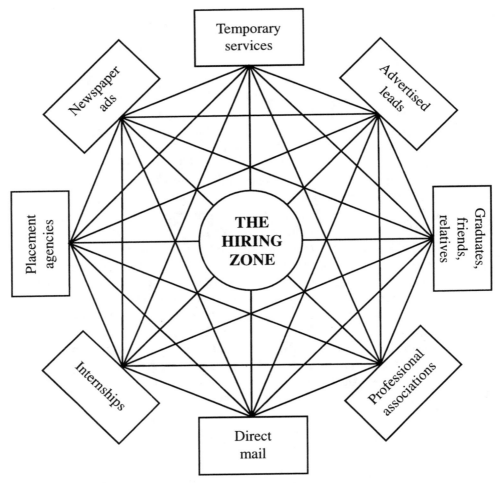

**Fig. 7-1**  The hiring zone.

## Direct mail

Using direct mail can help you discover unknown openings and get interviews in which you have little or no competition. People complain that direct mail is expensive and just a game of numbers, but they forget that if they "strike gold" by getting an interview for an unadvertised opening, they are going through the back door. Direct mail also has the feature of landing on advertised leads too. It gives you a forward momentum and the opportunity to gain a job without having to run through the formal advertised lead process competing with numerous candidates. Direct mail is the most panned, least appreciated, most magical of all synergistic job search tools. The cost must be considered, but the chief reason it is not utilized is because paralegals do not understand the theory of what they are doing. Most think that direct mail is like a Publisher's Clearing House approach, and your letter begins with "Hello, I am writing to every lawyer in the Western World." Instead, use the following steps to start an effective direct mail campaign:

a) Mail in small increments of 25 or less at a time to a select group.
b) Select a group (plaintiff personal injury firms in Littletown).
c) Craft a letter designed specifically for the select group, so that it does not *sound* like direct mail.
d) Do callbacks on your mailings.
e) Do follow-up mailings on positive responses. Go to interviews.
f) Repeat this process, group by group, in an organized, well-conceived program. Cover key towns and/or practice areas in a systematic fashion.

## Internships

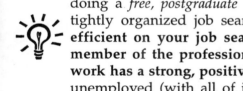

Some people like to build their resume and keep their skills honed by doing a *free, postgraduate internship*. Ten hours per week can fit into a tightly organized job search campaign. **Internships push you to stay efficient on your job search campaign and make you feel you are a member of the profession. Getting dressed up in a suit and going to work has a strong, positive psychological impact on you.** You don't feel unemployed (with all of its attendant negative ramifications). You also interview with greater confidence when you are asked about what you are doing now. Instead of saying, "I am unemployed and looking for a job," you can say, "I am currently working at Firm XY&Z on an internship to keep my skills sharp." The internship is also a place from which real jobs emerge. People are more likely to take a longer look at individuals. At some paralegal schools, up to half of the internships lead to some kind of temporary, part-time, or full-time permanent work. The internship is a way of getting inside the special world you are endeavoring to enter.

## Placement and temporary agencies

Many temporary placement agencies do permanent placements, and some permanent agencies have temporary departments. Note the difference, but be aware of the overlapping areas. Many agencies require experience before they will deal with you. In certain major cities though, entry paralegal candidates have been placed by placement agencies. It does not hurt to contact each placement agency in town to see if they will deal with you as a paralegal candidate. Many agencies are now developing "legal departments" to take advantage of the growth of the profession.

Temporary paralegal work, which is often litigation-support work, is an excellent way to get you over the entry-level hump. It enhances your resume, makes you money, and gets you into the legal world. An additional benefit is that it forces you to continue your hunt for a full-time paralegal job in an even more conscious and deliberate way; because you are working eight hours a day, your full-time job hunt must be super-efficient.

Temporary assignments can lead to full-time permanent work with litigation support and document management companies — a corporate, nontraditional growth area for paralegals. Litigation support duties, which include document review and coding and data entry, are often open to entry candidates. (Read the biographies in Chapter 8 and note what is stated about these kinds of jobs.)

Contact all the temporary services in your town and present yourself in the most professional manner you can. Keep your relationship with all agencies at a very high level: Burnt bridges to agencies are very difficult to rebuild. Do not fail to recognize the importance of these services to your career.

### Placement department leads

Your school undoubtedly has a job board and a career department of some kind. Stay in touch weekly with them and let them know of your interest and enthusiasm for legal placement assistance. Many graduates develop an "I'm-on-my-own-now" attitude. They let themselves feel cut off from the school after graduation and then do not take advantage of the services available to them.

### Graduates, friends, relatives

Once you have logged your names and contacted people, stay in touch with them. A friendly reminder every week or so keeps you in mind and lets them remember again that you need help. Log all of the activity you generate in your Journal of Professional Contacts so that you can keep track of the connections that you discover and the letters that you write.

### Newspaper ads

The synergistic job search is based upon the concept of connectedness. Read the entire newspaper and all of its ads. Business articles often foretell legal activity. Newly created legal job descriptions often emerge without the word "legal" in the title. Do not miss a week (or a day, for that matter) while you are in "search mode." When paralegals ask, "What should I look for?," the answer is, "Look for legal in other guises." The following list of job titles was garnered from a 1994 survey of paralegal graduates by the Denver Paralegal Institute. When you search through the Classified Ads, keep your eyes open to all kinds of possibilities.

Account Service Representative
Adjustor
Assistant Division Clerk
Associate Consultant
Bankruptcy Clerk
Case Manager
Closer
Closing Assistant
Compliance Administrator
Compliance Investigator
Contract Administrator
Contract Negotiator
Contract Legislative Analyst

Contract Paralegal
Corporate Practice Specialist
Data Entry Clerk
Enforcement Specialist
Executive Trial Assistant
Franchise Compliance Manager
Law Clerk
Legal Research Specialist
Legal Resource Analyst
Legal Technician
Legal Nurse Consultant
Manager of Administrative Services

Mediator
Medical Paralegal
Office Manager
Patent Administrator
Policy Audit Technician
Project Officer
Residential Closing Assistant
Restitution Officer
Risk Manager
Senior Loan Closer
Title Assistant
Trust Officer
Unit Manager

You put yourself in The Hiring Zone by doing everything at once. Of course you will find the lucky examples of people who did little and got work easily, often because they had the right connections. And of course you will see examples of people who work incredibly hard and seem to get nowhere. Neither of these extremes are reasons to not fully engage yourself in an all-out campaign to get a job.

## When My Crop Comes In—The Wait for Results

The truth about the job search process is that it takes a little while before you see results. Many job searchers complain that they see little fruit in the first part of the process, then turn around after several weeks and start talking about how three or four things came in on the same day. There is a *lag time* in this process. Contacts take time to mature. Openings take time to develop. The most successful and quick job results often consume weeks. Think of the simple analogy of bringing in a crop. There is plowing and digging and fertilizing and sowing and more fertilizer and rain and growth and maturity and hopefully more "rain in due season" and then—the harvest. None of these processes can be hurried. Farmers know that much of the job is doing and waiting and waiting and doing. You can't coax a crop out of the ground.

In the synergistic job search, you sow all kinds of seed as fast as you can in as many places as you can. The harvest comes in variously in different cycles. You do your best to do what you should at every turn (create, follow up, confirm, record, follow up, create, follow through). In all of this, however, there is the waiting. Once you have done *all* that you can, you have to stand back and let it grow. As much as we might like to, we cannot browbeat people into hiring us. You cannot talk an opening into existence and, most of all, you cannot make up a relationship that is not there in the first place. Remember in Chapter 3 the attitudinal elements to H.U.S.T.L.E.? Stay Cool, Let Things Work, and Expect Good News. These attitudes are as important as your actions. The synergistic job search depends upon understanding that *time* and *effort* work together.

## The Synergistic Job Hunting Success Scenario

When you move about in this little world of individuals, keep in mind that a valid informational networking approach is to ask for time or names or information. The people who go around asking simply for a full-time paralegal job will meet fewer people and get less help. If there is a job lying quietly in firm *E*, unannounced and unadvertised, just waiting to be discovered, and you are at firm *A*, what scenario will get you to *E*?

### Scenario #1: "Always Ask for a Job"
In this scenario, the only way you will get an interview is if you ask *A* for a job and then go blindly to *B* and ask for a job, and so on and so on until you stumble into *E*. No connection gets you to *E*, because you are always asking for a job. You are relying on luck and sheer persistence.

### Scenario #2: "Ask for Names and Information"
In this scenario, *A* does not have a job, but *A* refers you to *B* (because you ask for names and information). *B* does not have a job, but refers you to *C* (for the same reason). *C* refers you to *D* (because you ask for a name). *D* has a friend at *E* who knows about the unadvertised opening and gets you an interview. In this scenario, there is actually a path that the information flows along: *A*, *B*, and *C* did not know about *E*, but *D* knew *E* and *C*, and that is where the synergism came in. If you had not done the work of asking for names and information instead of a job, you would not have gotten the information until you hit *E* itself. Remember, *D* just knew *E*, *D* did not know *E* had a job opening.

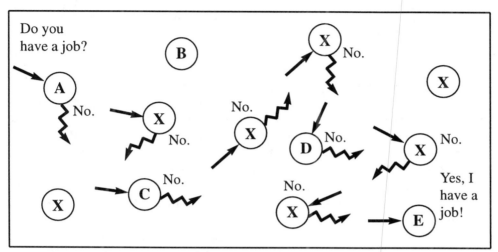

**Fig. 7-2** Scenario 1. Always ask for a job.

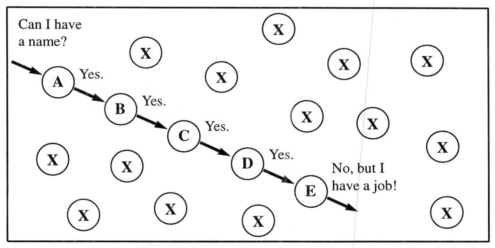

**Fig. 7-3** Scenario 2. Always ask for names and information.

## The Job That Is Filled Before It Is Open and the Unadvertised Job Opening

In cartoons, the artists communicate speed by drawing a cloud of dust instead of the character running. **In the world of hiring, there are openings that are only openings in name, for they will be filled before there is a spot to fill.** We all know about these kinds of openings in corporations, in which "Suzie from Accounting" is going to get that job.

### The Job That Is Filled Before It Is Open and the Unadvertised Job Opening

The job is announced and people are interviewed, but everyone knows "Suzie from Accounting" will get it. And then, before you know it, in the company newsletter an announcement appears. There's an opening in Accounting, formerly occupied by Suzie.

The reasons friendships are so important within your profession is that people in meetings at paralegal associations are often talking about exactly what you would like to know. In the inner world of paralegal synergistic connectedness, friends often arrange for other friends to be interviewed because people in the know are talking about openings that are about to occur. One woman in Jones, Jones and Smith is ready for a change. She hears that her friend at Doubleday and Brown is leaving. They sit down together and chat early on, the former recommending the latter. Often, the announcement of a willing candidate immediately follows the announcement of a departure. Sometimes management is just happy to hire because they are busy and the new person comes with a strong reputation. And thus one paralegal replaces another. Notice is given all the way around, and two people have quietly arranged the future for another. The more you can get on the inside of your professional world, the better off you will be.

All of the recommendations for a synergistic job search—the direct mail, informational interviewing, networking, joining associations, cultivating your personal group of friends share one very clear goal: You are seeking knowledge about unadvertised openings. **All of the methods and techniques of the synergistic job search are designed to reveal unadvertised openings.** If you do not see this clear goal, then you are like a runner who forgets that the race could eventually end, or a sailor who has lost a sense of that dry land he is headed for. Getting lost in the process can make you forget the why of all of these activities.

Advertised leads are said to represent about 20 to 25 percent of the total jobs available. That means that unadvertised leads constitute 75 percent to 80 percent of total openings, depending on the field you are discussing. Why is the job market like this? Because people want "quality control" over their applicants. They want to do as little interviewing as possible. (An advertised lead means lots of hours spent on resume review, interviewing, and candidate selection.) When people are forced to advertise, they do. There are many reasons why people advertise, but generally if people can hire a "friend" (networked through the back door), they will do it even after they have advertised publicly. This is a powerful mechanism. The sense of security that people have when they use "the back door" (network) is strong, especially when you counterbalance it against the apprehensiveness that accompanies hiring someone "off the street." It may not be fair, but it *is* human. When you fully engage in a job search campaign and you do it synergistically and with a totality of effort, you are automatically permitting all of these forces to carry you along instead of knock you over.

## Your Journal of Professional Contacts—The Job Hunting Notebook

The best job hunting efforts that are not properly recorded, logged, calendared, and "tickled" can prove fruitless. The person who does not feel the need to log and record all job search efforts is probably not doing enough of a job search. The first mandate is to record all of your contacts. Document all of the names you come across in your search. Put the names with firms or with other names.

There should be little need to persuade you to create a job hunting notebook: The professional paralegal understands implicitly the importance of documentation and not losing track of important facts. Besides, a synergistic job search demands this kind of attention after only a few days. Any job search that goes beyond a couple of weeks will get totally out of hand without some mechanism like a job contact book, a log, or at least a box or file cabinet in which everything is kept.

### Why keep a journal?

The need for a journal of professional contacts is never so keenly felt as when you answer the phone one morning just as you are wiping the sleep from your eyes. The voice on the other end is lively and bright. It seems that you wrote an excited and enthusiastic cover letter three weeks ago, and you were so persuasive about your desire for a real estate paralegal position that you truly convinced them that you have wanted to be a real estate paralegal since you were five.

You pause and take a deep breath. Your brain cannot remember the firm, the contact name, the job—even after they tell you who they are! "Well, yes, I remember writing you." You look down and on the table near the phone is your job log. You page through it quickly to your copy of the cover letter you sent three weeks ago. It all comes back, suddenly.

"Yes, I have been looking for a firm that could take advantage of my title experience; the title experience I mentioned in my letter was at an internship downtown." You restore yourself quickly and engage the caller like the fully "put together" professional that you are, standing there in your pajamas. This example has happened in real life, and it will continue to happen. The well-kept log can assist you in very real and immediate ways.

## Networking Analysis Worksheet

**NAME:** _____

**ADDRESS:** _____

_____

_____

**KIND OF MEETING (LOCATION, DATE, TOPICS, ETC):**

_____

_____

_____

**CONNECTION:**

_____

_____

_____

**HIRING STATUS:**

_____

**FOLLOW-UP PLAN:**

_____

_____

_____

## *Networking Analysis Worksheet*

A Networking Analysis Worksheet helps you keep track of who you met where and what you said to each other. Describe the important "connection" information. It will help you write a follow-up letter to that specific firm and that specific situation. The "status" tells you what you have told yourself to do regarding a connection. Some people do nothing with their connection. They neglect to write or call. Connections do not mean anything unless you include them in your synergistic search. Will you write to them? Will you call them? Are you waiting for them to do something? Did they tell you to write them in a month? Did they tell you to call them after the holidays? Whatever it is, give yourself something to do so that the connection will have value.

## *The Job Lead Sheet*

The Job Lead Sheet is an example of the kind of organization you might want to bring to the advertised leads to which you respond. Give yourself a place to paste in an ad, and then set up a series of objectives.

## *The Interview Fact Sheet*

With an Interview Fact Sheet you will be able to focus on the vital facts of the interview so you can keep control of your precious opportunity. Some people miss getting hired just because they forgot to focus on a specific issue in a certain interviewing setting. People lose job opportunities when they arrive late to an interview because they overlooked an important detail (for example, that parking was more complicated than they thought it would be). It would be tragic to lose a potential career position just because you forgot you had an interview at all.

## The Synergistic Networking Creed of the "Hire" Order

Read over the creed that follows. It focuses on the idea that you must be constantly mindful that your relationships and your connections are also the stuff of which your career will be made. **It is not simply what you have done and where you did it; it is who you knew while you were doing it and how you conducted yourself in the various places you worked.** Once you understand this, then you understand how opportunities emerge from people as well as from events, from relationships as much as from skills, from personal references as much as from titles and jobs.

The Synergistic Networking Creed of the "Hire" Order

**Job Lead Sheet**

**ADVERTISEMENT** (PASTE IN)

**Cover Letter Sent/First Contact Made:** Sent letter 3/15/94

**Response:** They said "no phone calls, please" so I must wait for their call. 3/23

**Call Back:** Got a message on my answering machine; called them to set up interview 3/26

**Interview:** Went on first interview. Thought I did well; may need to go over bio 3/29

**Thank You Letter:** Sent thank you card 3/30

**Further Activity:** Waiting for 2nd interview

**2nd Interview:**

**Result:**

**INTERVIEW FACT SHEET**

**Time:** 10:00 AM Monday 6/7

**Place:** Go down Broadway to First, turn right and park in the AAA Parking area, then walk two blocks to 342 Broadway

**Names:** Ask for Charlotte Jones

**Firm:** O'Leary Law Offices, one of three in metro area

**Expected Questions:** They will be looking for client contact skills since they are a debtor bankruptcy practice. Be willing to be a quick study in bankruptcy procedure. Study befor interview to get familiar with basic terms.

**Interview Outcome:** Thought I did well. I made second interview next week. Log 6/17 interview.

**Call Back:** Call and get Charlotte Jones' actual title

**Thank You Letter Sent:** Sent card to Charlotte and Mr. O'Leary

## THE CREED

> I realize that all contacts in my life can have some effect on me, and that many people still utilize contacts they made in their first job search. I realize that contacts, from whatever period in my life, might affect the next move I make or some future move I might make, and could benefit or harm me at a time in the future. I believe that I participate in this process for other people, consciously or unconsciously, to their detriment or benefit. I realize that this process works whether I am aware of it or not; but that my conscious and enlightened use of this networking creed will benefit myself and others in career fulfillment.

Never discount the human equation in your paralegal career. Some wonderful friends can be made at difficult legal settings. A person who was formerly unimportant to you can suddenly become essential to you. A person whom you found just marginally civil, but whom you treated with dignity and respect, could become the key connection in getting you into your next opportunity. We cannot overlook the dark side, either: Your worst enemy from your last job could end up a supervisor in your present job. Don't haunt yourself with this, but be mindful that while most of our relationships do not become vital to our future, we do not know which ones could.

## The human equation in law—protecting your paycheck through basic principles

Some simple principles have proven vital to the human equation in the law. When we attend to these principles, they "protect our paycheck." Think of how often these rules are violated and what you see as a debilitating effect, then consider these principles when they are positively followed and draw your conclusions about their benefit.

### Do Not Take Your Home to Work with You

Many will tell you not to take your work home, but most violate the former principle first. The first thing that happens to paralegals who get "comfortable" in their workplace is to get overly familiar. Ease erodes formality, and thus manners, and can degenerate into kidding and light insults, breeding overfamiliarity. It would be better if we respected one another and treated each other with dignity, but unfortunately, many people settle into an overt kind of "over-the-fence" gossipy quality that they feel makes them "like kin." Gossip, back-biting, political factions, personality conflicts, and other such negative circumstances emerge from a busy group of people when they allow this undignified familiarity to take over the tone of their professional relationships. Sharing your domestic grief, complaining about your home life, and moaning about your children's behavior are all ways in which we can quickly lose perceived value. It is a kind of self-undoing, but people justify it by saying, "This is the way the world works!" But true professional paralegals distance themselves from pettiness and back-biting and overly honest personal revelations. One of the essential paralegal qualities is the talent for diplomacy, that is, the ability to work on a team and be cooperative. When you allow interoffice communication and the tenor of your interoffice relationships to degenerate to the "familiar" and the base, then you are tarnishing your "professionalism." Ultimately, it is against self-interest not to be professional, but ironically, many fall prey to this human tendency.

### Take the High Road

This recommendation is multifaceted. It simply means that a paralegal succeeds with professionalism as his or her banner. Titles are not sufficiently weighty for the majority of paralegals to give them status, so always take the high road in your dealings with people and in meetings with associates, in lunches and in after-work encounters. Waiting until tomorrow to go on the record is often commendable. If you are required to defend yourself, do not be pleading and defensive. Take the high road. Do not get involved in "personalities." Say tomorrow what you could have said today, if it is possible. If you give way to anger, you will probably regret it, and you will be remembered for it. A written response to a serious situation is often recommended. When a verbal response is requested to a dramatic and difficult situation, blame and fingerpointing make you look weak and unprofessional. The shortest and most honest response is highly preferable to a ranting and accusatory defense. Take the high road in your socializing and in your use of humor and in "friendly kidding." Keep in mind that many things that seem to benefit you in the short term will hurt you in the long term.

### Do Not Burn Bridges

Unfortunately, many people conduct fairly professional lives and then "bite the hand that feeds them" when they are about to part company with a firm or friend or associate. When a very natural human tendency to release pent-up negative feelings takes over, they burn a bridge. They get their feelings off their chest, but have also ruined a relationship forever. It is very discouraging to look back at a firm and see scorched earth. If you have managed to get through an entire period of your career with certain unexpressed negative emotions, count yourself lucky and close off the relationship with a positive professional ending. Often a less than sterling relationship can be restored simply through the conscious use of a warm goodbye. Small social amenities are very powerful if used correctly. References, written and oral, are the lifeblood of the legal world. Prize them like precious mementos. Do not violate these basic rules of pleasantries and the formalities of good manners by letting go and venting. Remember, in the end, you are *protecting your paycheck.* Maybe the paycheck you are protecting is a paycheck you will receive five years from now. You never know!

The Synergistic Paralegal Job Search is truly the beginning of an interconnected web. You are just beginning and will always continue to weave and document this web of contacts, as long as you are making a livelihood as a professional paralegal. Your conduct and your skills and your awareness all blend together to make you a part of the Hire Order. The wonderful thing about paralegal career development is that after a few years your network is so well-developed that your second, third, and fourth jobs are arranged by you, for you, and with you and your network. Ask a paralegal with a well-developed network what they would do if they suddenly lost their job. Though it might be expressed in many different ways, that answer would sound something like this:

> If I suddenly lost my job? Hey, I'd call my top 20 friends and associates and have coffee and lunch and breakfast or whatever and I'd plug in my network and get it working for me. What do you think I've been doing for the last five years anyway?

## A Profession to Grow In

The paralegal profession is growing. The ranks of paralegals who are involved in corporations and government and traditional practices continue to grow. The person who succeeds in this profession understands that the value they have lies in their ability to continue to build skills and write a record of professionalism wherever they go. This is truly a profession; the paralegals who pioneered this profession should be congratulated for having a clear vision of the status that paralegals could achieve. You can follow the path of professional development. If you see your job as a career and not just a job, you will be well on your way to putting into practice the tools and techniques and strategies recommended in this book.

There seems to be an earnestness and seriousness in the people who want to become paralegals. This earnestness goes a long way toward making them successful. As it is with most things, it is the implementing of what you know works that makes the difference between success and failure. Your desire and commitment, if held strongly, will propel you into the synergistic job search, your subsequent professional paralegal development, and your network building.

When you immerse yourself in the hunt, it is always a good idea to rehearse the basics. Professional athletes and artists know that they must do this. Full immersion into such an occupying adventure occasionally requires perspective. So, the final recommendation of this book is rehearsal. Go back over the chapters of this book. Review the challenges you are facing, make notes and adjustments and then jump back into the fray. It is worth the effort!

# APPENDIX A

## *"Careers of Our Lives"*
### *Members of the "Hire" Order*

The profiles that follow reveal inside views of the variety of the paralegal profession. They show that this is one profession you don't have to be "stuck" in—it contains too much for one to feel trapped. These three profiles only begin to give a picture of the full variety that is the paralegal profession. Read and enjoy these stories.—Then go out and write your own.

### Career Profile: Lisa Rauhauser

*Author's Note:* Ms. Rauhauser's biography contains some good solid advice about the entry-level job search. She gives solid advice and insight into the prospect of establishing yourself as a paralegal. Her 12 years of experience give a full picture of what is indeed a challenging road with many possible turns. She also gives a snapshot of her vision of the future.

She talks practically about the flexibility one needs to "get on board" instead of holding to a fixed idea about a certain practice area. Many paralegals are concerned with how to make their past background translate into the legal profession. Ms. Rauhauser discusses this and other job search issues.

Her varied experiences, combined with a strong educational background, show a steady pattern of growth while she pursues her long-term goal. Her story also shows how "management skills" can be built all along the way and how being a paralegal means you are always engaged in on-the-job training. At the same time, as she points out, you can always direct your future.

## My first paralegal job: networking and the process of obtaining work

My first formal paralegal position was working for a major oil company in Los Angeles, California. My formal training includes an undergraduate degree in Liberal Studies from California State University, Northridge and an ABA Paralegal Certificate from the University of West Los Angeles. While my paralegal certificates were in Real Estate and Corporations, I worked in the Major Litigation unit of this major oil company's legal department. Finding this particular job was quite challenging, as my certificates were in the transaction side and not in litigation.

I always knew that I wanted to work in-house, as opposed to working in a law firm. As a result, I focused my job seeking effort toward corporate legal departments. I answered almost every classified advertisement in the local newspapers and legal journals for paralegal employment opportunities. I also registered with various employment agencies. I provided my resume to the Los Angeles Paralegal Association, which maintains a resume bank for employers who contact LAPA and are looking to hire paralegals. As a member of LAPA, I spoke to others in the organization and told them what type of work I was seeking. I also spoke with my professors and the career placement coordinator at UWLA.

Perhaps the most challenging aspect of my job search was that I had very little "formal" experience as a paralegal. This made the job search quite difficult. I received several responses from prospective employers indicating that since I did not appear to have any "traditional" paralegal experience they did not have an employment opportunity for me.

Besides answering ads to employers who had specific opportunities, I also decided to present my resume to corporations that I wanted to work for. This involved reviewing the corporate section of both the Martindale-Hubbell Law Directory and the Directory of Corporate Counsel in an effort to identify those companies with an in-house legal department. My whole job search included sending over 150 resumes to various employers. I received three interviews as a result. One was with a major oil company, where the initial interview involved meeting with four of their Senior Paralegals. My second interview involved meeting with the Director of Paralegals and the Human Resources Manager.

I knew that it would be difficult trying to get a job in a corporate legal department because there are fewer jobs in-house. Another obstacle that I had to overcome in selling myself to this particular employer was that I was still in paralegal school. Therefore, I had to sell my previous experience in a way that highlighted my abilities to perform paralegal work. Another hurdle was being able to represent that I could be a litigation paralegal even though I was studying corporate and real estate. I was eventually offered a position as a paralegal shortly after the interview with the Human Resources Department.

My litigation paralegal position with this oil company was challenging. Since I worked in the legal department's Major Litigation unit, I worked on very large-scale cases. My duties largely consisted of assisting the coordination and supervision of the litigation support activities for the cases I was assigned to. This was not a small task since the cases that I worked on involved productions of hundreds of thousands of pages of documents. I was specifically responsible for ensuring that the document productions were completed within given deadlines and supervising the staff involved. This meant analyzing the documents and ensuring that the appropriate documents were being produced or handled otherwise accordingly. Other duties included being involved in the creation of the databases for maintenance of documents.

As my past experience was in records management, I was also able to assist in the records management program while working as a paralegal. In this capacity, I was responsible for creating and maintaining indexes of inactive records and assigning retention dates of the documents. These skills were beneficial to my paralegal skills.

## *Entering the field: surprises and what I was unprepared for*

As I entered the paralegal field, I realized that while I had learned very specific concepts in paralegal school, my job as a paralegal encompassed much more. Specifically, my paralegal education did not include very important skills such as the use of computers and databases to manage massive amounts of documents. Technology changed rapidly, and I was not current. When I entered the field, scanning and imaging of documents had become a highly desirable means to house information. This was fairly new technology to everyone, so it was really a challenge to get myself educated in this area. I contacted vendors who supplied this type of equipment and obtained information from them. I also learned from hands-on experience. Had I been more educated in the use of automation in the legal field, I might not have felt so frustrated.

I was also unprepared for the job search itself and the time involved in interviewing. However, I found that being selective throughout my search provided me with the opportunity I was searching for. In all, it took me about six months to find my first paralegal position.

## *What I liked most about the paralegal field*

One of the most appealing parts of working as a paralegal was that there was always something to learn. You learn to work as a team player and can exceed your own expectations if you prove your abilities. Although a paralegal cannot practice law, one can certainly gain a high level of independence in his or her career.

Another thing I like is the flexibility; paralegals can branch into different areas, including management. The opportunities are diverse. For example, some paralegals are more experienced in performing legal research, while others are involved in litigation support including document management and analysis. Other opportunities are available to paralegals on the transactional side, where paralegals have worked in areas such as corporate and real estate. Experienced paralegals might find positions where, under the supervision of an attorney, they are actually managing cases and staffs. The level of independence can soar in certain environments. This made the paralegal profession appealing to me.

In addition to the different practice areas, paralegals have the option to pursue opportunities in various employment settings as well. For instance, a paralegal does not have to work in a traditional law firm setting. Other employers might include public and nonpublic corporate legal departments, governmental agencies, and financial institutions (to name a few). Again, this is another desirable aspect of the paralegal field for me.

## *Securing new employment and job changes: training in new areas and different office settings*

My professional experience includes not only working specifically as a paralegal but also as a Senior Records Administrator, Senior Records Systems Analyst, and currently as an Operations Manager for a temporary legal placement firm.

When I started out, the move to being a paralegal was a building block on my previous careers. Although it was discouraging at times, I think the career change was positive and beneficial. Moreover, as a paralegal I garnered not only my specific paralegal skills but also my management skills.

For example, since I worked in Major Litigation I dealt with cases that involved massive document productions. My ability to orchestrate such productions tested my management skills and improved my supervisory techniques. Not only were there attorneys on both sides of the litigation inquiring about various issues but there were all levels of personnel involved in the case, including litigation case clerks, paralegal assistants, and other paralegals. The productions often included meeting with nonlegal department personnel in an effort to identify documents and information that might be responsive to a particular case. As a result, I was able to further discover that I enjoyed the contact with a variety of people. This is one of the major reasons why I preferred to work in a corporation as opposed to a law firm: I enjoyed the contact with all levels of personnel in a variety of professions.

Before I became a paralegal, my previous positions involved paralegal skills. As Senior Records Administrator for the legal department of a nationwide manufacturer and retailer, I was responsible for managing all of the documents for the legal department and other departments as well. In this capacity I was required to analyze documents in order to categorize them appropriately for housing in the Records Center. I was required to ensure the safe housing of the company's charter documents. I also assisted with the due diligence projects that came about through the various acquisitions and divestitures, and in the maintenance and up-dating of the corporation's minute books and subsidiary minute books (which at one time included 250 companies). My legal research skills were also used. I was responsible for maintaining the law library and performed legal research both manually and on LEXIS/NEXIS as required by the law department staff and other employees of the corporation.

Likewise, much of my time working as a Senior Records Analyst for a national health care provider involved records management and paralegal skills as well. For example, a major portion of my time was spent managing documents and ensuring the retention of the documents. I researched the legal requirements for the retention of legal and nonlegal documents and made sure that our company was in compliance with the statutes regarding retention. I was also involved in identifying the inactive records that might be responsive to various requests for production generated by lawsuits involving the company. My interactions with employees at all levels was invaluable. I realized that I enjoyed the legal environment and decided to pursue a formal education in paralegal studies at the University of West Los Angeles.

It was a challenge to train in new areas of the law once I became a paralegal. Since my formal paralegal education was in corporate and real estate, I found myself receiving on-the-job training in litigation. While it was frightening and almost overwhelming, it was a positive experience. Not only was I challenged in the substantive areas with regard to learning new aspects of the law, I also found that each employment opportunity presented different physical settings. The most important thing that I learned in each new environment was to ask where things were located.

For instance, rather than spend time trying to locate the wordprocessing center, photocopy/duplicating center and mailroom, you should ask where these places are located. This will save invaluable time and much frustration in your first few weeks of employment. Likewise, you should find out how the firm or corporation tracks your time spent on various matters. Each employer is different and knowing how to account for your billable hours before you turn in an incorrect time sheet is essential.

After working as a paralegal for some time I realized that I really wanted to pursue my desire to work in Human Resources. Having learned from previous experience that searching for a job is in itself a full-time job, I decided to leave my job as a paralegal and to pursue my desire to work in Human Resources. I still required income, so I decided to register with a temporary legal placement firm so that I could work as a paralegal on a temporary basis. I was then given the opportunity to work for a firm on a temporary basis, assisting it with recruiting paralegals and attorneys on a project basis. I found that I truly enjoyed this type of work. I am now the Operations Manager of this placement firm. I am able to use much of my previous 12 years of experience in the legal field and at the same time continue to learn more about Human Resources. My customer services skills have been sharpened in that I deal on a daily basis not only with clients and potential clients but also our temporary legal staff and potential candidates. I have used this job change as another building block in my professional career.

## Overall impression of the paralegal field: past changes and future changes

My overall impression of the paralegal field is that it is a very competitive field for new graduates and experienced paralegals. In Los Angeles, many experienced paralegals are in the market looking for full-time regular positions. It appears to be an employer's market. This can be discouraging to new graduates or those with less experience, because many experienced paralegals are competing for positions that require less experience than they possess. In a better economic market they might not be pursuing these opportunities. I also see many paralegals accepting positions at lower pay than they would in a "good" market.

An alternative to the frustration of being out of work might include working as a paralegal on a temporary or project basis. This can be positive in that one gains paralegal experience and has some flexibility with regard to accepting an assignment. Some paralegals work solely on a project basis and make a career out of temporary work. Others work on a project basis until they are able to find full-time regular employment. I see more and more paralegals looking to project work as an alternative to regular full-time employment. The temporary work can involve very sophisticated projects. It is even possible for a project assignment to turn into a regular full-time position. Many employers view the project work as a good opportunity to look at the talent of various candidates and their work product. At the same time, the candidate can learn about the firm or corporation and decide if he or she is interested in pursuing the opportunity on a regular full-time basis. Project work thus benefits the client and the candidate. I see this type of work continuing to develop and grow in the future. Employers are now using project employees to assist with work overflows, and are benefiting in that they do not have to keep these employees as regular full-time employees on the books.

When I began my career in the legal field 12 years ago, the paralegal field was quite different. To begin with, I think there were more employment opportunities for paralegals. In fact, I think that some prospective employers were willing to hire a college graduate and train him or her as a paralegal. Today, I see that many perspective employers require not only an undergraduate degree but also a paralegal certificate from an ABA-accredited institution. I think that the future will continue to demand the same educational requirements.

Another change that I have seen in the industry includes that of automation. Many of the records once maintained manually are now being maintained in databases and spreadsheets. This is particularly evident with document management in large-scale litigation matters. Moreover, we are moving to an age of advanced technology involving imaging and scanning of documents. It would appear to be wise to keep up one's education on these technologies as well.

Overall, I see the future of the paralegal profession requiring the basic undergraduate degree and paralegal certificate in addition to continuing education in the field. Right now, we are seeing the debate over certification of our paralegals. I think that this shows the desire to continue to allow the profession to grow and develop. Also, I think if we continue to be educated with regard not only to the academic area but also the technical, we will keep up with the skills needed to be a successful paralegal in the 1990s and beyond.

## Career Profile: Richard H. Reich

*Author's Note:* I met Richard Reich at a National Association of Legal Assistants convention after hearing his presentation on the *Challenger* disaster and its subsequent litigation. Mr. Reich holds an important position in a successful law firm in North Carolina, but he also has an interesting story to tell about the road he took to get there. In his profile, read about the *Challenger* litigation, being a male in a female-dominated profession, and the effect of health problems on a career. Also, Mr. Reich discusses being out of the field completely for a period of time and having to reenter it.

Mr. Reich's portrait of an entry-level job is highly instructive and colorful. His story gives you a real picture of how deeply involving paralegal work can be, and why the work itself (especially litigation) provides a plethora of subject matter covering a world of topics. From dog bites to aviation disasters, the law can cover every area of life.

"We don't really know what a paralegal is supposed to do, but we'll hire you on a three-month trial basis and see if it works out." With that dubious acceptance, I began my paralegal career. It was February 1977, and paralegals were a new and fledgling breed among southern law firms. Yet the lawyers at Nelson, Mullins, Riley and Scarborough of Columbia, South Carolina were willing to explore the potential benefits of paralegal utilization. The three-month "trial basis" turned into three-and-a-half productive years as I helped that firm establish a growing paralegal section.

I first heard the term "paralegal" during my senior year as a Philosophy major at the University of North Carolina at Charlotte. A representative of the National Center for Paralegal Training (NCPT) was visiting the campus for a university-sponsored "Career Day" program, and I became intrigued by her description of the exciting possibilities associated with this new career. Having grown up enjoying the drama of lawyer Perry Mason and his assistant/investigator Paul Drake as they solved legal problems on television, I could see myself helping to put together the facts of a complex case that ultimately resulted in a victory for justice.

After I received my bachelor of arts degree with honors in the spring of 1976, I applied to NCPT and was accepted for its fall term. Upon my arrival in Atlanta that fall, I was surprised to find myself in the minority: There were far more female students than male students. The courses were unlike anything I had ever been exposed to. Classes ran Monday through Friday for almost the entire day with only a short break for lunch. Evenings were spent in preparation for the next day's classes. At that time, the school did not have a law library, so most of us would invade the Emory University School of Law library to complete our research assignments. The time I spent at NCPT was an invaluable learning experience that helped me establish a solid foundation of legal knowledge in civil procedure, legal research, corporate law, real estate law, and other general practice skills. The school also helped me prepare my resume and distributed it to law firms across the Southeast.

I received my Certificate from NCPT in January 1977 and immediately began the humbling process of trying to find employment. Initially, I was full of enthusiasm and great expectations about finding the perfect job. However, responses to my inquiries were slow to come. I followed any and all leads. My first few interviews in Virginia and the Carolinas were unproductive. Some law firms had no idea what paralegals were and were not the least bit interested in finding out. I gradually became concerned that this career was too new for most Southeastern law firms. If things were not bad enough, in late January I had a bout with kidney stones which put me in the hospital. It was during my stay in the hospital that I received a call from the Nelson Mullins firm wanting to know how soon I could come to Columbia, South Carolina to interview. I told them that I would be there as soon as the doctors released me.

On February 14, 1977, when I arrived for my first day of work at Nelson Mullins as a litigation paralegal, I had no office, desk, or telephone. Instead, I was assigned to a small table in a corner of the firm's library and worked out of my briefcase. After I survived the three-month trial basis, a small, windowless storage room was cleared out and it became my office, complete with a desk, chair, and telephone. My initial assignments were to locate and interview witnesses in connection with minor traffic accidents, prepare summaries of those interviews, summarize depositions, and draft simple interrogatories and other simple pleadings. I did not have a typewriter, wordprocessor, or a secretary. Instead, I was given a dictation machine and instructed to utilize the secretary for the attorney who had assigned me the work. This did not go over well with some of the secretaries, who saw me as an interloper in their domain. I quickly developed diplomatic skills to mollify the secretaries' displeasure and to assure that my work got done.

As I gained more experience and confidence, the challenges increased. I never said no to an assignment and many times found myself in waters that were over my head, but the lawyers at Nelson Mullins were mostly supportive (although I can recall being called on the carpet on more than one occasion for some type of screw-up). The bad experiences were just as valuable as the good ones in helping me grow in my chosen career; I am just happy that they were not as numerous.

As the attorneys gained confidence in my abilities, they would assign me more sophisticated cases to work on, including medical malpractice and product liability cases. Some administrative duties were also assigned, such as docket control and court calendar call. During the next couple of years, the firm prospered and grew. The offices moved to a high-rise office building and my new office had a window. As the firm added new attorneys, it also added paralegals, and one of my duties was to assist with hiring new paralegals. I now received packets of resumes from NCPT similar to the packets in which my own resume was included only a few years earlier. In October 1980, I married, and my wife and I decided to return to my hometown of Winston-Salem, North Carolina to start our family. I left my good friends at Nelson Mullins on the best terms and with their good wishes for my success.

Once settled in Winston-Salem, I worked for about a year as a salesman and assistant manager with my family's wholesale building supply business. By February 1982, my efforts with an employment agency obtained me an interview with the Petree Stockton law firm, one of the oldest and most respected firms in North Carolina. Petree Stockton had an established paralegal section with paralegals in most areas of its practice. My interview went well and on January 11, 1982, I began my first day as a litigation paralegal with Petree Stockton. I was initially assigned to the insurance defense group, where I worked on cases similar to those I had worked on at Nelson Mullins.

In 1984, I was assigned to work with the firm's product liability and aviation litigation group. It was my association with this group that ultimately resulted in my involvement with the space shuttle *Challenger* litigation.

On Tuesday, January 28, 1986, at 11:38 a.m., the flight of the space shuttle *Challenger* began. It ended 73 seconds later in a violent explosion. All seven crew members perished. The investigation and subsequent litigation that arose following this disaster consumed much of my life for the next three years. At the time of the *Challenger*'s launch, I had been working with attorney William F. Maready for a little over two years. Mr. Maready was the senior partner who headed Petree Stockton's product liability and aviation litigation group. He was also a close, personal friend of Captain Michael J. Smith, who was an officer in the U.S. Navy and the pilot of the ill-fated spacecraft.

Soon after the accident, Captain Smith's widow, Jane, sought the help of her husband's lawyer friend. Once he was retained as counsel for the Smith family, Mr. Maready quickly assembled the "Shuttle Group." The core of this group was composed of four lawyers and the one paralegal—me. Assignments were distributed and we set about the arduous task of preparing a case against the National Aeronautics and Space Administration (NASA) and solid rocket motor manufacturer Morton Thiokol, Inc.

During the course of the litigation, I became familiar with the basic operations and components of the space shuttle and was involved in a wide variety of projects. Included among those projects was extensive research of Morton Thiokol's corporate history and status, research at the National Archives and Records Administration of the records generated during the Presidential Commission's investigation of the accident, and preparation of document requests to NASA pursuant to the Freedom of Information Act.

The reports, records, and photographs obtained from the Archives and NASA were a gold mine of evidence that provided us with a solid foundation on which to build our case. However, those records were incomplete in many respects and it was only through the painstakingly difficult and often hotly contested discovery process that we were finally able to piece together the series of events that led to and eventually caused the disaster.

Marshaling the avalanche of documents, legal pleadings, and other materials fell to me. With the help of my trusty computer, I devised a data management system to help with the analysis of all these materials. The system later proved to be invaluable as we prepared for depositions and for trial.

During the course of the litigation, the U.S. district court dismissed the Smith family's claim against NASA. It based its decision primarily on the *Feres* doctrine, which basically says that a serviceman is not entitled to sue the government. The court of appeals upheld the decision, and a petition to the Supreme Court was denied.

As trial approached, the only defendant left was Morton Thiokol. Our group now shifted into high gear in preparation for trial: Trial motions and briefs were prepared; witnesses and exhibits were designated; video-taped depositions were excerpted for the jury to view. I had even reserved hotel accommodations for our trial team. In general, the entire trial machine was fine tuned and readied for what we expected to be a long and fiercely contested trial.

On August 22, 1988, both parties came together with the judge to have all pretrial motions heard. What happened next was unexpected. After nearly two years since the *Challenger* accident, Morton Thiokol was now ready to seriously negotiate a settlement of the case. Thus, on the eve of trial, the case was resolved. The Court ordered that all settlement documents be sealed.

After the shuttle case, I continued to work primarily with Mr. Maready on other product liability and aviation cases, including a claim arising out of the airline disaster that occurred in Sioux City, Iowa. I also became more involved in the North Carolina Paralegal Association, Inc. and served as Chairman of its Board of Directors from 1989 until 1991, having received its Outstanding Service Award in 1990.

In 1992, my world was shaken when Mr. Maready and several other lawyers decided to leave Petree Stockton and start a new law firm. I had to decide whether to go with them or stay put. It was a very hard and emotional choice. I ultimately chose to stay with Petree Stockton.

At first, I was apprehensive about my choice, but am now convinced that it was for the best. After the departure of Mr. Maready and the others, I requested to be reassigned to the firm's environmental law practice group. My experience with toxic tort product liability cases provided a natural bridge into this relatively new practice area. However, I found that there was much for me to learn about the highly technical and constantly changing environmental laws and regulations. I welcomed the challenges and continue to be invigorated by the new subject matter and responsibilities. Although I have fond memories of the years spent with my departed attorney friends, I do not regret the decision I made to stay with Petree Stockton. I accepted the change as an opportunity to broaden the scope of my knowledge and abilities. I have not been disappointed.

My career as a paralegal has for the most part been very rewarding and fulfilling. I continue to enjoy being a part of this growing and dynamic profession, and foresee a bright future for those who choose it as their own career.

## Career Profile: Terri Robinson

*Author's Note:* Terri Robinson, the Director of National Accounts for Interim Legal Personnel, began her career with a "short-term temp" assignment. She stumbled upon a growing profession several years ago and then was required to get the education she needed to continue in her profession. Even though she holds a responsible national position today, her story really isn't about high pay and glory. It's about flexibility, doing what's put in front of you happily, and then seeking your own path. Ms. Robinson's story is about being willing, being able, and then just working hard.

I have quite a paralegal story to tell, and it begins with taking a "temp job." Before I go back to the beginning, I'll talk about where I am in the present. I work for Interim Legal Personnel, a personnel service that specializes in placing paralegals, attorneys, and litigation-support personnel on temporary projects or in full-time positions in law firms and corporate law departments. Interim also has other law-related services, such as transcript summarizing and court reporting services. Since we had the national capabilities, coupled with the multiservice lines, we wanted to focus on our competitive advantages. My position and division were created with a "national scope" in mind. I am responsible for tying it all together and marketing our "national package" to potential major accounts.

I hold a national marketing position now, but my actual paralegal experience prepared me for it. In fact, it was a career in its own right, for the paralegal job description itself became an outline for my key to success.

As I look back, it seemed all quite accidental. Seriously, at the time I didn't even know what a paralegal was. But I was in the right place at the right time, and to give myself some credit, I recognized an opportunity when I saw it, and then pursued it. Doing that led to my getting official paralegal training. When I look at this job, and then how I got started as a paralegal, I realize my entire career is *ironic*. I took a one-month temporary job with the Carnation Company with supposedly no future that ended up lasting *nine years*. A temporary assignment was the beginning of my paralegal career.

I went to Carnation to fill in for the Labor paralegal, who was leaving to study for the Bar. I had no legal background at all. But I picked up on things quickly, and didn't really need to know anything about paralegal work to just keep things moving until the paralegal returned. I worked for the General Counsel and for the Labor/Employment Law attorney. I took to the environment like a fish to water. I really enjoyed it. And I loved the people at Carnation. I felt at home. When the paralegal returned to work, the company had another opening in Real Estate. They asked me if I would extend my assignment until they could hire someone.

I spent the next two months in Real Estate. The attorney was great to work with, but I did not enjoy the practice area as much. After those two months they offered me a full-time position in Real Estate. I was going to take it, but at the same time the Labor paralegal decided that while she was waiting for bar results, she was going to tour Europe. I decided I *really* wanted the Labor position, so I applied for it. The General Counsel was interested, but the Labor attorney wanted me to have legal training. He was really hung up on that. So I suggested that I take a paralegal class as a condition of employment. He hired me; I took the class. Then I decided to complete the paralegal certificate program, and I did—with honors, if I can blow my own horn—at the University of Southern

Career Profile: Terri Robinson

California. At that time they had an ABA-approved program. And *that's* how I became a paralegal!

I stayed with Carnation/Nestle for nine years. My specialty was Employment and Labor law. After Nestle acquired Carnation, the attorney I worked with was promoted to Vice President of Corporate Human Resources and Management. I transferred with him as the HR Dept. Administrator. We kept our law practice and assumed the company's entire HR function on top of that. A most interesting time! When my position was restructured, it was decided that Labor/Employment law belonged back in the Legal Department. I didn't want to go back to the Legal Department, and I was overqualified for the new Human Resources job, so it was time for me to move on.

After such a great career and all the time I spent at Carnation, I was a little upset that my job was eliminated. You never think such a thing could happen to you. But after the shock wore off, I looked at it as an incredible opportunity. I wouldn't admit it at the time, but I was starting to get bored with my job. There weren't any more challenges. I knew that I had gone as far as possible in that environment. But I was so comfortable there, I would not have actively sought another job. So after the restructuring, I realized it was actually a blessing in disguise. Carnation gave me a very fair severance package, which allowed me to take my time to make sure the next career step was the right one. I wasn't pressured to take just any job to pay the bills. I had the opportunity to explore, and ultimately make a great career choice. It was the best thing that could have happened to me.

The job I sought became the position I now hold. My days are interesting and varied. Typically, the day starts at home at about 6:00 a.m., when I can catch my East Coast clients at the beginning of their day, before the pace gets hectic. Then I get to the office about 9:00 a.m., where it's more of the same. When I'm in the Los Angeles office I spend most of my time on the phone talking to people that might have a need for our services.

When I am on the road, things are quite different. It's quite stressful. Two things make it so. First is the internal stress from my position in the company, because my performance is measured in part by how much new business I generate, then by repeat business, and of course, my profitability. I think I am good at what I do, so I don't worry about it all the time, but it is in the back of my mind. Then there's the external stress. Can you imagine the pressure when a client calls on Friday to say that they need 30 people to work the weekend on a document review in Phoenix? It is pressure for me to find 30 qualified people for the project in the time constraints that exist. I admit that I get "creative" at times. It's amazing. But let me take you back to the start.

When I look back on my career with Interim, I have covered a lot of ground. I have been with Interim for almost eight years in various positions. As my talents in marketing developed, I basically grew into this position. So it was a logical step for me in my career development. I have held several different positions since I started in 1986. The company was beginning to examine the field of niche staffing businesses. Our upper management team scanned the services being offered in the marketplace, and noticed "paralegals" were being provided on a very small scale. Fortunately, someone recognized that this was a "hot career"; the synergy between the legal field and the personnel services industry could make a whole new division for our company. They tested the theory by hiring an attorney to create a business plan. That is where I came in. They made Los Angeles a test market, and I was hired to manage the company's first "stand-alone" legal office that would cater exclusively to law firms and corporate law departments. It was a prototype office; depending on how well we did, so would go the future of the division.

I had been "restructured out" from my job at Carnation/Nestle and was working at various temporary/part-time jobs. One job was at a recording studio, which was full of interesting people. It was fun to see how that field operates. But as time went on I decided to get back into the legal area again, so I started a serious job search. Interim was running an ad for a "paralegal with sales, marketing, and management experience to manage" their new Los Angeles office. I had a strong paralegal background in employment and labor law, and experience as department administrator. Then, too, I had retail sales, which I hoped could stretch to meet the sales and marketing requirements. So I sent in my resume. I interviewed and got the job!

Yes, it is a sales position now. It's funny; no one in the legal field likes to have anything to do with sales. They think it has a negative connotation. Some attorneys are in sales, but would never admit it. The way I see it, everyone is in sales in some way. We all have something to sell, whether it is ourselves or a special program that we want to implement. Parents "sell" to their children, and vice versa. Life is all about selling and persuasion. Granted there are different styles, and fortunately my style is both compatible and appropriate for the legal field. My style is professionally aggressive, but low-key and unthreatening. I focus on a consultative approach and on building relationships.

But aside from a natural ability for sales, my paralegal experience was the most important factor in landing this job. In order to have credibility when placing paralegals, it is important to have the technical knowledge about what paralegals do in the law office environment. In addition, we are still educating a lot of attorneys about how to utilize paralegals effectively. But it was also important from a recruiting standpoint. Paralegals consider themselves professionals and want to be treated that way. The traditional agencies just didn't know what paralegals were or did. Interim understands the paralegal profession; we can make good client/candidate matches. Since we had all of these goals, we accomplished quite a lot.

Soon, we acquired another paralegal service in Los Angeles and merged our offices. At the same time we set up other legal specialty offices in New York, Boston, Washington, D.C., Detroit, and Chicago. Then we opened new offices in San Francisco and Philadelphia. We also made several important acquisitions in New York and Minneapolis. That basically brings us to this point in time.

I have always felt my paralegal training and experience could stand on their own or be a stepping-stone to something else. I always believe that opportunities exist—I just have to keep an eye out for them. I took the job at Interim because it looked like a great challenge and opportunity and would ultimately offer great rewards. I had nothing to lose and everything to gain, so I was willing to try. I had the paralegal certificate and experience and the right personality type. I tried to emphasize that I had an old-fashioned work ethic. Also, I have a good sense of humor, which is always an asset, and I didn't try "to hold up the store" in salary requirements. I knew I had a lot more to gain by making an investment in my future; a reasonable salary traded off for training and experience in this new field. I'm grateful that my manager saw me as a "diamond in the rough," but it has been a mutually rewarding association. The company has benefited and my hard work has paid off for *me*, too.

This job will definitely keep me busy for at least two more years. This is a very exciting time at Interim. We have just been spun off from our former parent, H&R Block. Interim is definitely growing, so there could well be other interesting opportunities for me right here, if that's what I want. Right now, I'm very satisfied with my career track with Interim.

To think it all started out when I *accidentally* became a temporary paralegal! I got the necessary paralegal training, made it through several transitions, and just kept at it. This profession is doing the same thing for thousands of paralegals across the country. It can provide a whole array of exciting challenges, and give not only a great career, but also a great chance to make a contribution in the legal profession.

# APPENDIX B

## Professional Associations

### ALABAMA

Alabama Association of Legal
   Assistants
c/o Pamela Gray
Capell, Howard, et al.
P.O. Box 2069
Montgomery, AL 36197

Legal Assistant Society of Southern
   Institute
c/o Mr. Chris Christ
Paralegal Progam—Southern Institute
2015 Highland Avenue South
Birmingham, AL 35205

Mobile Association of Legal Assistants
c/o Mary Beth Bradley, President
P.O. Box 1852
Mobile, AL 36633

### ALASKA

Alaska Association of Legal Assistants
P.O. Box 101956
Anchorage, AK 99520-1956

Alaska Legal Assistants Association
P.O. Box 1956
Anchorage, AK 99510

Fairbanks Association of Legal
   Assistants
c/o Rebecca J. Saluri
Law Offices of Daniel T. Saluri
P.O. Box 75090
Fairbanks, AK 99707

Juneau Legal Assistants Association
P.O. Box 22336
Juneau, AK 99802

### ARIZONA

Arizona Association of Professional
   Paralegals
P.O. Box 25111
Phoenix, AZ 85002

Arizona Paralegal Association
c/o Pat Steiner
Jennings Stouss & Salmon
One Renaissance Square
Phoenix, AZ 85004

Legal Assistants of Metropolitan
   Phoenix
c/o Alexis D. Buiroz
Snell & Wilmer
1430 Valley Bank Center
Phoenix, AZ 85073-3100

Northern Arizona Paralegal
  Association
Dept. of Law Enforcement & Paralegal
  Studies
Northern Arizona University, Box
15005
Flagstaff, AZ 86011

Southeast Valley of Legal Assistants
c/o Sandy Slater
423 N. Country Club, #50
Mesa, AZ 85201

Tucson Association of Legal Assistants
c/o Barbara Tidd
1319 S. Lynx Drive
Tucson, AZ 85713


**ARKANSAS**

Arkansas Association of Legal
  Assistants
Cathie Cox
Wright, Lindsey & Jennings
2200 Worthen Bank Building
Little Rock, AR 72201


**CALIFORNIA**

California Alliance of Paralegal
  Associations
114 Sansome Street, #644
San Francisco, CA 94104

Central Coast Legal Assistants
P.O. Box 93
San Luis Obispo, CA 93406

Central Valley Paralegal Association
c/o Frances M. Foxen
Thayer, Harvey, Hodder & Gregerson
City Mall 948 Eleventh Street, Suite 20
P. O. Box 3465
Modesto, CA 95353

Coalition for Paralegal and Consumer
  Rights
1714 Stockton Street, Suite 400
San Francisco, CA 94133

Inland Counties Paralegal Association
P.O. Box 292
Riverside, CA 92502-0292

Legal Assistants Association of Santa
  Barbara
c/o Lynn Mollie
Henderson & Angle
530 E. Montecito Street
Santa Barbara, CA 93103

Los Angeles Paralegal Association
P.O. Box 241928
Los Angeles, CA 90024
(818) 347-1001

Marin County Association of Legal
  Assistants
P.O. Box 13051
San Rafael, CA 94913-3051

NAPA Valley Association of Legal
  Assistants
Wagner Hamilton & Associates
1836 2nd Street
Napa, CA 94559

Orange County Paralegal Association
P.O. Box 8512
Newport Beach, CA 92658-8512

Paralegal Association of San Mateo
c/o Linda Vetter
250 Wheeler Street
Redwood City, CA 94061

Paralegal Association of Santa Clara
  County
c/o Donna Rowson
1864 Mohican Court
Fremont, CA 94539

Redwood Empire Legal Assistants
P.O. Box 1498
Santa Rosa, CA 95402

Sacramento Association of Legal
  Assistants
P.O. Box 453
Sacramento, CA 95812-0453
(916) 763-7851

San Diego Association of Legal
  Assistants
P.O. Box 87449
San Diego, CA 92138-7449
(619) 491-1994

San Francisco Association of Legal
  Assistants
P.O. Box 26668
San Francisco, CA 94126-6668
(415) 777-2390

San Joaquin Association of Legal
  Assistants
P.O. Box 1306
Fresno, CA 93715

Sequoia Paralegal Association
P.O. Box 93278-3884
Visalia, CA 93278

Ventura County Association of Legal
  Assistants
c/o Sheree Thompson
1210 Escalon Drive
Oxnard, CA 93030

## COLORADO

Legal Assistants of Colorado
c/o Alma Rodrigues
4150 Novia Drive
Colorado Springs, CO 80911

Rocky Mountain Legal Assistants
  Association
P.O. Box 304
Denver, CO 80201
(303) 369-1606

## CONNECTICUT

Central Connecticut Association of
  Legal Assistants
P.O. Box 230594
Hartford, CT 06123-0594

Connecticut Association of
  Paralegals — Fairfield County
P.O. Box 134
Bridgeport, CT 06601

Connecticut Association of
  Paralegals — New Haven
P.O. Box 862
New Haven, CT 06504-0862

Legal Assistants of Southeastern
  Connecticut
P.O. Box 409
New London, CT 06520

## DELAWARE

Delaware Paralegal Association
P.O. Box 1362
Wilmington, DE 19899

## DISTRICT OF COLUMBIA

National Capital Area Paralegal
  Association
1155 Connecticut Avenue, N.W.
Washington, D.C. 20036
(202) 659-0243

## FLORIDA

Broward County Paralegal Association
c/o Leigh M. Williams
Ruden, Barnett, McClosky, et al.
P.O. Box 1900
Ft. Lauderdale, FL 33302

## Appendix B. *Professional Associations*

Dade Association of Legal Assistants
c/o Priscella Meyer
700 Bricknell Avenue
Miami, FL 33133

Florida Legal Assistants, Inc.
c/o Nancy A. Martin
P.O. Box 503
Bradenton, FL 34206

Jacksonville Legal Assistants
c/o Teresa Arington
7751 Belfort Parkway, Bldg. 200
Jacksonville, FL 32216

Orlando Legal Assistants
c/o Roxane MacGillivray
Akerman, Senterfitt & Eidson
P.O. Box 231
Orlando, FL 32802

Pensacola Legal Assistants
c/o Deborah Johnson
Levin, Middlebrooks, & Mabie
226 S. Palafox Street
Pensacola, FL 32581

### GEORGIA

Georgia Association of Legal Assistants
P.O. Box 1802
Atlanta, GA 30301
(404) 433-5252

### HAWAII

Hawaii Association of Legal Assistants
P.O. Box 674
Honolulu, HI 96809

### IDAHO

Idaho Association of Legal Assistants
c/o Joanne Kimey
P.O. Box 1254
Boise, ID 83701

### ILLINOIS

Central Illinois Paralegal Association
c/o Melanie Baker
1700 North School — #88
Normal, IL 61761

Illinois Paralegal Association
P.O. Box 8089
Bartlett, IL 60103-8089
(708) 837-8088

Independent Contractors Association of
Illinois
6400 Woodward Avenue
Downers Grove, IL 60516

### INDIANA

Indiana Legal Assistants
c/o Dorothy French
Newman, Trockman, et al.
P.O. Box 3047
Evansville, IN 47730

Indiana Paralegal Association
P.O. Box 44518, Federal Station
Indianapolis, IN 46204

Michiana Paralegal Association
P.O. Box 11458
South Bend, IN 46634

### IOWA

Iowa Association of Legal Assistants
c/o D. Diane Smith
310 Strawberry Lane
Ames, IA 50010

Paralegals of Iowa, Ltd.
P.O. Box 1943
Cedar Rapids, IA 52406

## KANSAS

Kansas Association of Legal Assistants
c/o Ronda R. Hoover
Pizza Hut, Inc.
9111 E. Douglas, P.O. Box 428
Wichita, KS 67201

Kansas Legal Assistants Society
P.O. Box 1675
Topeka, KS 66601

## KENTUCKY

Lexington Paralegal Association
c/o Edwina Gilmore
P.O. Box 574
Lexington, KY 40586

Louisville Association of Paralegals
P.O. Box 962
Louisville, KY 40201

## LOUISIANA

Baton Rouge Paralegal Association
P.O. Box 306
Baton Rouge, LA 70502

Louisiana State Paralegal Association
c/o Wanda V. Courmier
P.O. Box 1743
Lake Charles, LA 70602

New Orleans Paralegal Association
P.O. Box 30604
New Orleans, LA 70190

Northwest Louisiana Paralegal
  Association
c/o Cheryl Mahaffey
610 Marshall Street, Suite 212
Shreveport, LA 71101

Southwest Louisiana Association of
  Paralegals
P.O. Box 1143
Lake Charles, LA 70602

## MAINE

Maine Association of Paralegals
c/o Lawrence Yerxa
McEachern & Thornhill
P.O. Box 360
Kittery, ME 03904

Maine Association of Paralegals
Southern Maine Chapter
P.O. Box 7554 DTS
Portland, ME 04112

## MARYLAND

Baltimore Association of Legal
  Assistants
P.O. Box 13244
Baltimore, MD 21201

## MASSACHUSETTS

Central Massachusetts Paralegal
  Association
P.O. Box 444
Worcester, MA 01614

Massachusetts Paralegal Association
P.O. Box 423
Boston, MA 02102
(617) 469-7077

Western Massachusetts Paralegal
  Association
P.O. Box 30005
Springfield, MA 01102

## MICHIGAN

Legal Assistants Association of
  Michigan
c/o Cora S. Webb
P.O. Box 12316
Birmingham, MI 48012

Macomb Community College
c/o Cheryl L. Jensiewski
Legal Assistant Program
14500 Fourteen Mile Road
Warren, MI 48093

## MINNESOTA

Minnesota Association of Legal
  Assistants
8030 Old Cedar Avenue
Suite 225
Bloomington, MN 55425
(612) 853-0272

Minnesota Paralegal Association
c/o Tracy Blanshan
Kennedy Law Office
724 SW First Avenue
Rochester, MN 55902

St. Cloud Area Legal Services
c/o Mary Yeager
P.O. Box 896
St. Cloud, MN 56302

## MISSISSIPPI

Gulf Coast Paralegal Association
942 Beach Drive
Gulfport, MS 39507

Mississippi Association of Legal
  Assistants
c/o Connie M. Cavanaugh
Wise, Carter, Child & Caraway
P.O. Box 651
Jackson, MS 39205

Mississippi University for Women,
  Student Chapter
c/o Teresa Dunser
809 Second Avenue, North
Columbus, MS 39701

Paralegal Association of Mississippi
P.O. Box 22887
Jackson, MS 39205

Society for Paralegal Studies
University of Southern Mississippi
c/o Laura Lilly
S.S. Box 5108
Hattiesburg, MS 39406-5108
(601) 266-4310

## MISSOURI

Gateway Paralegal Association
P.O. Box 50233
St. Louis, MO 63105

Kansas City Association of Legal
  Assistants
P.O. Box 13223
Kansas City, MO 64199
(913) 381-4458

Northwest Missouri Paralegal
  Association
Box 7013
St. Joseph, MO 64507

St. Louis Association of Legal
  Assistants
c/o Carol Young
P.O. Box 9690
St. Louis, MO 63122

Southwest Missouri Paralegal
  Association
c/o Marie E. Smith
517 East Seminole
Springfield, MO 65807
(417) 887-7890

## MONTANA

Big Sky Paralegal Association
P.O. Box 2753
Great Falls, MT 59403

Montana Paralegal Association
c/o Clare Young
P.O. Box 693
Billings, MT 59103-0693

## NEBRASKA

Nebraska Association of Legal
   Assistants
c/o Linda A. Walker
McGill, Gotsdiner, Workman & Lepp,
   P.C.
10010 Regency Circle, Suite 300
Omaha, NE 68114

## NEVADA

Clark County Organization of Legal
   Assistants, Inc.
c/o Robin S. Orwiler
Edwards, Hunt, Hale & Hansen Ltd.
415 S. 6th St., Suite 300
Las Vegas, NV 89101

Nevada Paralegal Association
c/o Robin S. Orwiler
Edwards, Hunt, Hale & Hansen Ltd.
415 S. 6th Street, Suite 300
Las Vegas, NV 89101

Sierra Nevada Association of
   Paralegals
c/o Carol A. Hunt
P.O. Box 40638
Reno, NV 89504

## NEW HAMPSHIRE

Paralegal Association of New
   Hampshire
c/o Frances Dupre
Wiggen & Nourie
P.O. Box 808
Manchester, NH 03105

## NEW JERSEY

Central Jersey Paralegal Association
c/o Barbara McManus
Rutgers, The State University of New
   Jersey
Office of Employment & Labor Counsel
60 College Avenue
New Brunswick, NJ 08903

The Greater New Jersey Paralegal
   Association, Inc.
P.O. Box 805
Edison, NJ 08818-0805

Legal Assistants Association of New
   Jersey
c/o Dorothy Deignan Perretti
Dwyer, Connell, Lisbona
427 Bloomfield Avenue
Montclair, NJ 07043

New Jersey Legal Assistants
   Association
Central Jersey Paralegal Division
P.O. Box 403, US Highway 130
Dayton, NJ 08810

Paralegal Association of Burlington
County College
P.O. Box 2222
216 Haddon Avenue
Westmont, NJ 08108

Paralegal Association of Central Jersey
93 Princeton Court
Mercerville, NJ 08619

South Jersey Paralegal Association
P.O. Box 355
Haddonfield, NJ 08033

**NEW MEXICO**

Legal Assistants of New Mexico
c/o Jacque Walston
The Modnoll Firm
500 45th Street
Albuquerque, NM 87103

**NEW YORK**

Adirondack Paralegal Association
c/o Maureen T. Provost
Bartlett, Pontiff, Stewart, Rhodes &
    Judge, P.C.
One Washington Street, Box 2168
Glen Falls, NY 12802-0012

Legal Professionals of Dutchess County
c/o Terri Thorley
51 Maloney Road
Wappingers Falls, NY 12590
(914) 897-4100

Long Island Paralegal Association, Inc.
P.O. Box 31
Deer Park, NY 11729

Manhattan Paralegal Association
200 Park Avenue, Suite 303 East
New York, NY 10166
(212) 986-2304

Paralegal Association of Rochester, Inc.
P.O. Box 40567
Rochester, NY 14604

Southern Tier Association of Paralegals
P.O. Box 2555
Binghamton, NY 13902

Westchester County Paralegal
    Association
c/o Connie Vincent
Law Offices of David E. Worby, P.C.
Two Lyon Place
White Plains, NY 10601

Western New York Paralegal
    Association
P.O. Box 207
Niagara Square Station
Buffalo, NY 14202

Westrock Paralegal Association
c/o Debby Ybarra
Box 101
95 Mamaroneck Avenue
White Plains, NY 10601

**NORTH CAROLINA**

Coastal Carolina Paralegal Club
c/o Elisabeth Alvarez-Fager
5634 Delaware Avenue
Camp Lejeune, NC 28542

Cumberland County Paralegal
    Association
P.O. Box 1358
Fayetteville, NC 28302
(919) 323-4111

North Carolina Paralegal Association
c/o Gayle D. Green
Route 2, Box 711
Denver, NC 28037

Raleigh Wake Paralegal Association
P.O. Box 1427
Raleigh, NC 27602

Triad Paralegal Association
Drawer U
Greensboro, NC 27402

## NORTH DAKOTA

Red River Valley Legal Assistants
c/o Jeanine Rodvold
Conmy, Feste, Bossart, et al.
400 Norwest Center
Fargo, ND 58126

Western Dakota Association of Legal
  Assistants
c/o Janie Eslinger
McGee, Hankia, et al.
P.O. Box 998
Minot, ND 58702

## OHIO

Cincinnati Paralegal Association
P.O. Box 1515
Cincinnati, OH 45201

Cleveland Association of Paralegals
P.O. Box 14247
Cleveland, OH 44114
(216) 575-6090

Greater Dayton Paralegal Association
P.O. Box 515
Mid City Station
Dayton, OH 45402

Legal Assistants of Central Ohio
P.O. Box 15182
Columbus, OH 43215-0182
(614) 224-9700

Northeastern Ohio Paralegal
  Association
c/o Joanne Vetter
265 South Main Street
Akron, OH 44308

Toledo Association of Legal Assistants
c/o Karen Breener Wasil
Owens-Illinois, Inc.
One Seagate
Toledo, OH 43699

## OKLAHOMA

Oklahoma Paralegal Association
c/o Denise Newsom
McKnight & Gasaway
P.O. Box 1108
Enid, OK 73702

Rose State Paralegal Association
c/o Marisa Ann Bruner
1811 Wren, #3
Norman, OK 73969

Student Assn. of Legal Assistants
Rogers State College
c/o Leslie Fuller
RR3, Box 12A
Beaver, OK 73932

TJC Student Association of Legal
  Assistants
TJC-Legal Assistant Program
c/o Judith Tucker
909 S. Boston, Room 429
Tulsa, OK 74119

Tulsa Association of Legal Assistants
c/o Stephanie Mark
Hall, Estill, et al.
4100 BOK Tower
Tulsa, OK 74172

## OREGON

Oregon Legal Assistants Association
P.O. Box 8523
Portland, OR 97207
(503) 796-1671

Pacific Northwest Legal Assistants
c/o Jana Bauman
Swanson & Walters
975 Oak, Suite 220
Eugene, OR 97401

## PENNSYLVANIA

Berks County Paralegal Association
c/o Daniella Johnson
Roland & Schlegal
P.O. Box 902
Reading, PA 19603-0902

Central Pennsylvania Business School
Student Legal Assistant Association
c/o Peggy Clements
Campus on College Hill
Summerdale, PA 17093

Central Pennsylvania Paralegal
Association
P.O. Box 11814
Harrisburg, PA 17108

Lancaster Area Paralegal Association
c/o Rosemary Merwin
Gibble, Kraybill & Hess
41 East Orange Street
Lancaster, PA 17602

Northeastern Pennsylvania Association
of Legal Assistants
c/o Brenda K. Harvey
Hourigan, Kluger, Spohrer & Quinn
Conyngham-Drums Road
RR 1, Box 464
Sugarloaf, PA 18249-9737

Paralegal Association of Northwestern
Pennsylvania
P.O. Box 1504
Erie, PA 16507

Paralegal Association of Peirce Jr.
College
c/o Peirce Junior College
1420 Pine Street
Philadelphia, PA 19102

Pennsylvania Business Institute
Paralegal Association
13 Armand Hammer Boulevard
Pottstown, PA 19464

Philadelphia Association of Paralegals
1411 Walnut Street, Suite 200
Philadelphia, PA 19102
(215) 564-0525

Pittsburgh Paralegal Association
P.O. Box 2845
Pittsburgh, PA 15230
(412) 642-2745

Sigma Pi MU—Legal Assistant
Division
c/o Marywood College
Social Science Department
P.O. Box 704
Scranton, PA 18509

Wilkes-Barre Area Group
c/o Tom Albrechta
6 East Green Street
West Hazelton, PA 18201

York County Paralegal Association
P.O. Box 2584
York, PA 17405-2584

## RHODE ISLAND

Rhode Island Paralegal Association
P.O. Box 1003
Providence, RI 02901

## SOUTH CAROLINA

Carolina Paralegal Association
c/o Anna Chason
7437 Highview Road
Columbia, SC 29204

Charleston Association of Legal
   Assistants
c/o Stacie Rose
Stuart Feldman, Esq.
P.O. Box 429
Charleston, SC 29402

Columbia Legal Assistants Association
c/o Barbara G. McGui
McNair Law Firm, P.A.
P.O. Box 11390
Columbia, SC 29211

Greenville Association of Legal
   Assistants
c/o Gail White Nicholson
Wyche, Burgess, Freeman & Parham
P.O. Box 10207
Greenville, SC 29603

Paralegal Association of the Pee Dee
c/o Martha Knight
P.O. Box 5592
Florence, SC 29502

## SOUTH DAKOTA

South Dakota Legal Assistants
   Association
c/o Cindy Johnson
8801 Woodland Drive
Black Hawk, SD 57718

## TENNESSEE

Cleveland State Community College
Legal Assistant Association
P.O. Box 3570
Cleveland, TN 37311

Middle Tennessee Paralegal
   Association
P.O. Box 198006
Nashville, TN 37219

Memphis Paralegal Association
P.O. Box 3646
Memphis, TN 38173-0646

Southeast Tennessee Paralegal
   Association
c/o Calecta Veagles
P.O. Box 1252
Chattanooga, TN 37401
(615) 756-7000

Tennessee Paralegal Association
c/o Sandra M. Hughes
Albert W. Secor, P.C.
600 Georgia Avenue, Suite 8
Chattanooga, TN 37402

## TEXAS

Alamo Area Professional Legal
   Assistants, Inc.
P.O. Box 524
San Antonio, TX 78292

Capital Area Paralegal Association
c/o Chris Hemingson
Pope, Hopper, Roberts & Warren, P.C.
111 Congress, Suite 1700
Austin, TX 78701

Dallas Association of Legal Assistants
P.O. Box 12533
Dallas, TX 75225
(214) 991-0853

El Paso Association of Legal Assistants
c/o Angela Tanzy
2610 Montana
El Paso, TX 79903

Fort Worth Paralegal Association
P.O. Box 17021
Ft. Worth, TX 76102

## Appendix B. *Professional Associations*

Houston Legal Assistants Association
P.O. Box 52241
Houston, TX 77052

Legal Assistants Association/Permian
  Basin
c/o Cecile Wiginton
P.O. Box 913
Midland, TX 79702

Legal Assistants Division of the State
  Bar of Texas
P.O. Box 12487
Austin, TX 78711

Legal Assistants Professional
  Association (Brazos Valley)
c/o Linda Manning, Acting President
P.O. Box 925
Madison, TX 77864

Northeast Texas Association of Legal
  Assistants
c/o Genee McFadden
3704 Kriss Drive
Longview, TX 75604

Nueces County Association of Legal
  Assistants
c/o Diane De La Garza
1100 First City Tower II
Corpus Christi, TX 78478

Southeast Texas Association of Legal
  Assistants
c/o Janie Boswell
P.O. Box 813
Beaumont, TX 77704

Texarkana Association of Legal
  Assistants
c/o Debbie H. Brower
Holeman, Arnold & Cranford
2222 Hampton Road, Box 5367
Texarkana, TX 75505-5367

Texas Panhandle Association of Legal
  Assistants
c/o Nancy Stephens
P.O. Box 1127
Amarillo, TX 79105-1127

Tyler Area Association of Legal
  Assistants
P.O. Box 1178
Tyler, TX 75711

West Central Texas Association of
  Legal Assistants
P.O. Box 6902
Abilene, TX 79608

West Texas Association of Legal
  Assistants
c/o Eyvonne Crenshaw Palmer
P.O. Box 1283
Brownfield, TX 79316

Wichita County Student Association
c/o Kathy M. Parker Adams
Continued Education
Midwestern State University
3400 Taft
Wichita Falls, TX 76308

## UTAH

Law Society
c/o Legal Assistant Program
Utah Valley Community College
1200 South 800 West
Orem, UT 84058

Legal Assistants Association of Utah
c/o Max Bullett
Moyle & Draper
15 East First South
Deseret Plaza Building
Salt Lake City, UT 84111

## VIRGINIA

Peninsula Legal Assistants, Inc.
c/o Diane Morrison
Jones, Blechman, Woltz & Kelly, P.C.
P.O. Box 12888
Newport News, VA 23612

Richmond Association of Legal
  Assistants
c/o Vicki M. Roberts
McGuire, Woods, Battle & Boothe
One James Center, 5th Floor
901 E. Cary Street
Richmond, VA 23219

Roanoke Valley Paralegal Association
P.O. Box 1018
Roanoke, VA 24005
(703) 982-8000

Shenandoah Valley Paralegal
  Association
c/o Nancy Bryant
P.O. Box 88
Harrisonburg, VA 22801

Tidewater Association of Legal
  Assistants
c/o Claire S. Isley
Willcox & Savage, P.C.
1800 Sovran Center
Norfolk, VA 23510

## WASHINGTON

Columbia Basin College Paralegal
  Association
c/o Peggy Cottrell
Westinghouse Hanford Company
P.O. Box 1970
Richmond, WA 99352

Washington Legal Assistants
  Association
2033 6th Avenue, Suite 804
Seattle, WA 98121
(206) 441-6020

Washington State Paralegal Association
P.O. Box 232
Ardenvoir, WA 98811
(509) 784-9772

## WEST VIRGINIA

Legal Assistants of West Virginia, Inc.
c/o Mary Pat Hanson
Hunt & Wilson
P.O. Box 2506
Charleston, WV 25329-2506

West Virginia Association of Legal
  Assistants
c/o Ms. Paula Houston
Volk, Frankovitch, Anetakis, Recht,
Robertson & Hellerstedt
3000 Boury Center
Wheeling, WV 26003

## WISCONSIN

Paralegal Association of Wisconsin
P.O. Box 92882
Milwaukee, WI 53202
(414) 272-7168

## WYOMING

Legal Assistants of Wyoming
c/o Nancy R. Hole
Brown & Drew
Casper Business Center, Suite 800
123 West First Street
Casper, WY 82601

Wyoming Legal Assistant Association
c/o Roger Thomas
HC 31, Box 2746H
Riverton, WY 82501
(307) 856-0814